Rituals to the Ten Archangels

black&white interior

by Maha Vajra

Planned, composed and written by a human,
with ai-assisted correction and rewriting tools.

F.Lepine Publishing

© François Lépine, 2024

ISBN: 978-1-926659-50-3

www.TenArchangels.com

Table of Contents

What are Archangels

An angel is considered to be a single local entity (one individual angel). An archangel is a universal archetype, not a single entity. An archangel is a consciousness that pervades the entire universe with its wisdom, knowledge, and frequency. In other words, angels are the individual spirits you could have a conversation with, even if you have the impression it doesn't answer. The archangel would then be the sum of all angels of its type. Angels and Archangels do not answer with words, but with influence. They affect your life positively as you cultivate a relationship with them.

When you speak, pray, or do a ritual to an archangel, your thoughts, intentions, and consciousness transmigrate into the archangel's realm, or range of consciousness frequency, or field of consciousness. From there its own consciousness modulates your plea, and it is returned to you, charged with the archangel's own universal wisdom and power. Speaking openly to an archangel might have a small effect. Dedicating time to prayer will have a medium effect. Doing a ritual to the archangel will yield the most powerful effect.

Each archangel has a range of affinities, or types of wisdom it can convey back to you. Here we will describe the 10 major archangel s, so you can know what type of help you can get from them all. It is also useful to strengthen your bond with the archangels, nourishing your relationship with them, simply to receive their general blessings in your life.

The universe we inhabit is a dynamic and complex system, filled with various physical and spiritual forces that animate and shape its very fabric. These forces are responsible for the motion of celestial bodies, the behavior of subatomic particles, the functioning of living organisms, and the evolution of consciousness. In this chapter, we will explore some of the key physical and spiritual forces that animate our universe.

Physical Forces

While this book is about archangels, we still want to provide a basic set of laws of physics, since they inherently are the physical manifestation of their spiritual counterpart. Physical forces are the fundamental interactions that govern the behavior of matter and energy in the universe. They are described by mathematical equations and are measurable through experiments and observations. There are four known physical forces that are recognized by modern physics: gravity, electromagnetism, strong nuclear force, and weak nuclear force.

Gravity is the force that attracts two masses towards each other. It is the force responsible for the motion of planets, stars, and galaxies. It is a long-range force, meaning that its effect can be felt over large distances. At least, that is the layman explanation. Gravity is also known in the field of quantum physics, as a force that molds the fabric of space and time.

Electromagnetism is the force that governs the behavior of electrically charged particles. It is responsible for the behavior of light, electric and magnetic fields, and the interactions between charged particles. Electromagnetic force is also responsible for the functioning of electronic devices, such as computers and cell phones.

The strong nuclear force is responsible for holding the nuclei of atoms together. It is a very short-range force and is much stronger than electromagnetism or gravity.

Without this force, the universe would consist of nothing but scattered protons and neutrons.

The weak nuclear force is responsible for some types of radioactive decay. It is a short-range force and is much weaker than the strong nuclear force. It plays a major role in the inner functioning of atoms. Each of these processes are irrelevant to, and too complicated for the scope of this book.

Spiritual Forces

Spiritual forces are often thought of as intangible, non-physical energies that animate the universe. They are often associated with religious or mystical beliefs and are not measurable by scientific instruments. However, many people believe in the existence of spiritual forces and their influence on the physical world.

To give an example, one of the most universally recognized spiritual forces is the concept of qi (pronounced "chee"), which is central to Chinese medicine and martial arts. Qi is believed to be the vital life force that animates all living things, and its flow through the body is said to be essential for good health and well-being.

Another spiritual force that is widely recognized is prana, which is central to yoga and Ayurvedic medicine. Prana is believed to be the universal life force that permeates the entire universe, and its proper flow through the body is believed to promote good health and spiritual development.

In many traditional cultures, there is a belief in a spiritual energy that flows through the natural world. This energy is often referred to as mana, and it is believed to be present in all living things, as well as in natural features such as mountains, rivers, and trees. Many indigenous cultures believe that by connecting with this energy, one can gain access to spiritual guidance and healing.

In many religious and spiritual traditions, angels are viewed as powerful forces that exist within the universe. Angels are often described as divine messengers, intermediaries between the divine and human realms. They are believed to possess spiritual powers that enable them to guide, protect, and heal humans, and to influence events in the physical world. Angels are also thought to be present in the natural world, guarding over animals and plants and helping to maintain the balance of the ecosystem. While the existence and nature of angels is a matter of belief and faith rather than scientific observation, their presence in many different cultures and religions speaks to the profound impact they have had on human consciousness throughout history.

The physical and spiritual forces that animate our universe are complex and interdependent. While physical forces are measurable and describable by scientific methods, spiritual forces are often based on subjective experiences and beliefs. However, both types of forces are essential for understanding the universe and our place in it. By exploring and understanding these forces, we can gain a deeper appreciation of the complexity and beauty of the universe we inhabit.

Historic records

Angels and archangels have been present in human culture for centuries. They have been portrayed in various forms and contexts, reflecting the diverse beliefs and traditions of many civilizations. Yet, before humanity came to be, these archangelic forces existed in the universe, simply they were not named or conceptualized before a humans could name them. They are archetypes that maintain the structure of the spiritual world, and they affect the physical world.

The first angels are believed to have originated in ancient Mesopotamia where they were viewed as divine beings that served as intermediaries between gods and humans. In the Hebrew Bible angels played a significant role as messengers of God, delivering divine messages to prophets and serving as protectors of the faithful.

As Christianity emerged in the Mediterranean world, angels became a part of Christian theology. The New Testament refers to angels as messengers of God and servants of Christ, and they are often depicted as benevolent beings who guide and protect humans. During the medieval period, angels became a central theme in Christian art and literature, often depicted with wings and a halo. In addition to their traditional roles as messengers and protectors, they were also seen as warriors in the fight against evil.

In Islamic tradition angels are called "Malaika" and are viewed as servants of God who carry out his commands. They are believed to have been created from light and have various duties, including recording the deeds of humans and guarding the gates of paradise.

In Hinduism, angels are known as "Devas" and are viewed as celestial beings who possess supernatural powers. They are often associated with the gods and goddesses of Hindu mythology and are believed to play a role in maintaining the balance of the universe.

In the modern era, angels have remained a popular subject in art and literature, and have been the focus of numerous books, movies, and television shows. The concept of guardian angels, in particular, has gained widespread popularity, with many people believing that they have a personal angel who watches over them and protects them from harm.

Archangels, on the other hand, are a distinct class of angels that are believed to have greater power and authority than regular angels, mainly because they are not individuals, but universal concepts.

The historic records of angels and archangels reveal a rich and diverse cultural legacy, with these celestial beings playing a prominent role in the beliefs and traditions of many civilizations. Whether viewed as messengers, protectors, or warriors, angels have captured the imagination of humans throughout history and continue to inspire and fascinate us today. In this book, we will focus mostly on the Kabbalistic aspect of angels and archangels.

Building the Relationship

Before having a conversation with anyone, it can be useful to know their name, unless it is a mundane chat with someone you'll soon forget. To delve into a deeper conversation, someone's name might not be enough; knowing more about that person helps. It is the same with an archangel. To deepen your connection with an archangel, you must contemplate not only its name, but it's purpose, or function.

We use the name of an archangel to focus our feelings, our intention, into a state of being. The study and meditation of a name will attune you to its true nature.

The names of the archangels are in Hebrew. Each of them has a simple definition, but there is more to it. Each letter has a numerical value, and a basic intention, which explains it's influence once we combine them. It is not the focus of this book to delve deep in *notarikon* and *gematria*, but the serious occultist might want to study these two topics. We will provide sufficient information for you to build your relationships with the archangels.

Developing a good relationship with someone we wish to collaborate with is an essential aspect of achieving success in many fields, from business to science, to art. A strong bond built on trust and mutual respect can lead to a more efficient, productive, and fulfilling collaboration, which can bring significant benefits to both parties involved.

When individuals work together, they bring their unique skills, perspectives, and experiences to the table. However, without a solid foundation of trust and communication, misunderstandings and conflicts can arise, leading to wasted time, resources, and even damage to the project's outcome. On the other hand, when collaborators trust and respect each other, they can openly share their ideas, provide constructive feedback, and work together to find creative solutions to challenges that may arise.

In addition to improving the collaboration's quality, a good relationship with a collaborator can also lead to long-lasting benefits, both with humans or archangels. Collaborators who work well together can build a network of professional connections, share knowledge and expertise, and even start new ventures together.

Such relationships can lead to opportunities for future collaborations, partnerships, and friendships, which can enhance personal and professional growth.

Understanding vs. Feeling

The difference between understanding a concept, and feeling a state of being is fundamental in developing an occult skillset. Too much in your head, and you'll be locked in controlled knowledge that will prevent all the subjective aspects of the experience. Too much in your heart or guts, floating on a river of feelings and excitement, you'll easily get lost in dreams of your own invention, losing track of the objective results you wish to produce.

It is crucial to the occult experience, to have a proper intellectual understanding of the concepts exposed in this book. It is also important to remain available to what will be reveal, which is the supernatural aspect of the occult experience.

The mental work invested will focus your mind on the forces you want to get in touch with, and give you the understanding of the inner mechanics of rituals. It then belongs to the mystical side, filled with inspiration, that revelations will come. One of the goals of doing rituals is to learn something more than a book can teach you. It is to focus on a source of wisdom, for then that source to fill you with it's concepts, through revelations.

If you rarely, or never allow yourself to feel things, finding comfort in the mind, a pressure builds up inside that eventually will have to come out. We too often find it reassuring, the impression that we can control everything with a proper understanding. That is a false sense of security that denies the inevitable entropy of life. We can never be really certain about all things. Life will show us that not everything goes according to a plan.

The first stage in developing your relationship with an archangel starts with empowering its name through a meditative practice, through which you'll bind that name to what you have learned of the archangel, and over time, cultivate the state of being embodied by that archangel.

You'll be using your intellect to acquire and remember the most important aspects of each archangel. Then, you'll be using your heart to patiently allow the archangel to imprint you with its consciousness.

Empowering Their Names

You can start doing prayers and rituals before empowering their names. Actually, you should start right away. But if you are serious about this work, and wish for their more powerful interventions, we recommend the simple following practice.

First, read the entire chapter about each specific archangel, so that during your meditation, you'll be able to ponder the concepts they represent. For each name of the 10 archangels, meditate on them 20 minutes in a row, for 10 days. During this meditation, we recommend you whisper or recite at low voice the name of the archangel you are charging. If you wish to give this archangel access to your physical reality, you should have a minimal physical aspect to your meditation. If you skip a day, it's not dramatic, but if you skip more than one, you have to start the process, resetting your daily counter for that archangel. When you meditate, recite the name in your mind if you must, or whisper it softly, every 5 to 10 seconds. Focus on its intention, its base feeling (each explained in The Archangels section). Try to reach a state of being, your mind dwelling on what you've learned of this archangel.

We recommend you start with Metatron, the 1st archangel, and follow the list in order. You can take a few days pause between each archangel, if you want. Once you have empowered an archangel's name in you, that empowerment is fixed in you for a long, long time. And it will be maintained as long as you sporadically do spiritual practices.

Empowering an archangel's name:

- Sit comfortably in a relatively silent place, not lying down
- Select the archangel's name and refresh your mind with its concept
- Meditate on it 20 minutes per day, every day, for 10 days
- Proceed to the next archangel

This empowerment process would indeed require 100 days. You can shorten that period by combining two per day, at separate times (i.e. one in the morning, one in the evening). While you meditate, you should repeat the name of the archangel in your mind every few seconds. You can even whisper is one in a while. This will help your mind stay on the meditation.

Can I do 200 minutes in a row and just be done with it? The short answer is: no. When you go to the gym to lift weights, doing 200 repetitions of a heavy lift won't give you the same results as doing 20 repetitions per day, for 10 days (day off every other day for a physical exercise on a muscle group). Your body needs time to build the new muscle mass and the nerve connections. In the case of meditative empowerment, your mind needs the day, focusing on other things, to reinforce the connection. It's like having muscles in the mind. Doing 20 minutes per day for 10 days is enough to build a good relationship with the archangel.

You can meditate with your eyes closed. You can start by gazing at the image of the archangel for the first minute, then close your eyes. The most important aspect is reaching the state of being, the feeling of the intention. You'll get this through practice.

If your mind won't stop, the empowerment still works if you spent at least that time doing the practice. Try your best to spend as much of the 20 minutes on the archangel. But a human mind has its own subconscious will, and it likes to dwell on random topics, what it desires, or events what troubles you in more dramatic times. It's ok. Meditation is not meant to shut down your mind, or keep it concentrated constantly. That feat is practically impossible without a decade of training. Find peace in meditation, and simply bring your mind back to the contemplation when you realize you had lost it.

If you transcend -- the impression of falling asleep or losing consciousness -- the empowerment still works; you haven't lost your day. Transcending happens when the higher vibrations you are invoking are affecting your mind. You should still feel refreshed after a good transcending meditation.

Sitting is the best position for meditation. Lying down can easily make you actually fall asleep, which is not the same as transcending. Sleeping can make you lose your daily charge. But worry now, you don't have to start everything over. Just add a day to your charge if you had fallen asleep for most of the period.

The Major Archangels

We will now name the 10 major archangels and describe their concept. You should re-read each chapter once before starting your 10 days charging meditation.

For each of them, we will start with an inspiring poetry, followed by a more technical and metaphysical description. The poetic story is meant to inspire you to feeling the archangel's state of being, while the technical part wishes to satisfy your intellectual needs of structure and understanding.

Following the romantic, then technical presentation, we will provide Correspondences, which will be better understood and used during the rituals. These correspondences comprise name in Hebrew letters, the color, numerology, gematria, favored period, and area of influence (applications). An in-depth understanding of the Archangels will allow you to better select which one you wish to invoke for which purpose. But if you fails to find the Archangel that works best for your desired application, we will provide later in the book, an exhaustive list of modern interpretations for each Archangel's field of application.

We will also provide an image meant to inspire you. At the end of the book, you will find 2 copies of each image, with a cut line, for you to remove from the book and use during your rituals or prayers. Thes images are ideal for using as a main focus in the center of your altar, during your rituals.

It is known by many occultists that there are symbols and images associated with the archangels. We will abstain from providing such symbols for the main reason that they have all been created recently, in the past centuries, most in the past decades, and do not really reflect the concepts that we are using in this book, since we are based on old kabbalistic methods. We recommend you use the name in

Hebrew letters as the main symbols for your rituals and prayers. It is not required to use angelic symbols for these rituals. This book not being specifically about Kabbalah, and that it would take hundred of hours just to explain the Hebrew alephbeith (alphabet), we provide the written name only, without details or etymology.

1- Metatron מַטַטְרוֹן

Inspiration

Moments before creation, the archangelic abstract concepts, just, happened. They filled the universe as it was being made. The first of these archetypal mechanics of creation, was Metatron. He represents the event that caused all intangible plans to become their manifested version.

Metatron is the passing from the non-existent to the solid thing. From concept to object. From energy to mass. From the first plane of the creator, he manages the densification of conscious intentions, making them pass through all planes of consciousness, until they reach the physical plane of reality.

Metaphysics

In quantum mechanics, geometry is different than what you've learned at school. It is a concept hard to see. Space and time seem to fade away into a mix of chances and changes. If we describe a shape using a formula, we can think of space and time being shaped by that formula until a result appears, bringing something real into existence. As we look deeper, we see that these changes are not completely random. They form a pattern that shapes the universe.

Quantum geometry is a difficult but interesting part of physics. It shows the strange nature of reality at its deepest level. However, people in esoteric or mystical fields often use these terms loosely. We want to avoid using too much scientific language in this book, which is focused on subjective ideas.

Quantum geometry doesn't have a fixed shape. It's like a sea of endless possibilities, filled with every possible version of space and time, yet never settling on one. It's a delicate balance between potential and reality, showing how the universe is full of limitless possibilities. This constant back-and-forth between what could be and what is makes quantum geometry hard to fully understand but also fascinating.

This geometry isn't made of points and lines like in regular math. It's made of consciousness, ideas with an intention but without form. Quantum geometry is no a set of shapes, but an abstract plane where ideas and plans try to conceive all their possible future form.

What seems like empty space or a vacuum, is actually full of activity. Particles and antiparticles constantly appear and disappear in a cycle of creation and destruction. This happens not just in our universe but across all 10 levels of consciousness, where the archangels exist.

This process is called quantum fluctuation. It's the concept where matter and mass comes into being. This is how Divine Consciousness, which wants to experience itself, will become solid as it turns into physical matter. It's like a unformed consciousness, filled with the desire to know and understand what it is, that makes up a world for which to come into existence.

The 10th plane of consciousness is the physical world where things can be observed and experienced. Here, traditional physics applies. Once particles are formed in this plane, they interact with each other, creating the matter we see in the universe. So, what seems like empty space is actually full of matter and energy, all starting from quantum fluctuations.

Metatron is the archangel who symbolizes the thickening of energy and consciousness into solid matter. When you meditate on Metatron's name, think of how the universe forms from nothingness, becoming real and solid.

Correspondence

Name: Metatron

Hebrew: מַטַּטְרוֹן

Color: White to represent manifestation, black to represent its origin in vacuity.

Numerology: 1

Gematria: 964
M 40, t 9, t 9, r 200, o 6, n 700

Planet: The universe, the primordial fire

Favored period:
Sunrise for manifestation
midnight for vacuity and access to the origin
Any day of the week and month

Applications:
Communion with God
Feeling the Creator in your life
Transcendental meditation
Manifestation without precision (no specific plan or object of desire)
Manifestation, humility, paradoxes

Metatron מַטַּטְרוֹן

2- Ratziel רָזִיאֵל

Inspiration

Ratziel represents the highest mysteries of life and the universe. Most would think that the greatest mysteries are occult in nature and mysterious, like magic formulas and abstract geometry. In fact, the greatest mysteries are the mysteries of life, the simple mysteries that we face ourselves during every experience.

Ratziel as often being seen as a source of deep mystical revelations on how to pray or do rituals or obtain favors from God, actually it is the science of self observation and personal growth to an extreme that it becomes a spiritual practice.

The mysteries that you encounter in life are a function of being exposed to the hardships and the joy that you have to process and gain simple life wisdom from. Understanding how it feels to go through this or that experience, is the key to unlocking the secrets of Ratziel. Every time you have a present or every time you have a heartbreak, you get to learn more about what life is about. This is where the study of razia starts but not where it ends.

As you grow into personal growth and deep spiritual understanding, you will get to learn mysteries that transcended the human mind as they start to relate to your soul. Ratziel Will eventually reveal to you the mysteries of the divine, but only has you have processed the mysteries of handling a simple humble human life.

Metaphysics

As we start to understand the mysteries of the occult, it's important to see that the hidden knowledge we seek is closely connected to the mysteries of life itself. The way to understand these occult mysteries is not just by studying symbols and rituals. It is by learning more about ourselves and doing personal growth.

The occult is a type of knowledge that is kept secret and hidden from those who are not initiated. It deals with magic, mysticism, and spirituality, giving deep insights into how the universe works. This hidden knowledge can change how we see the world, showing us how everything is connected and revealing the nature of existence.

Life's mysteries can be quite deep. It takes patience, dedication and perseverance to progressively unlock the secrets of the universe. It involves lots of learning, lots of time spent practicing, and observing the subtle changes in our lives, as a result. The human mind is very complex. The universe is so vast. From the microcosmos to the macrocosm, great fields are yet to be explored and understood.

Studying the occult pushes us to grow as a person. It makes us face our fears, our emotions, our beliefs. It confronts us with a world that is not born of the human mind. This can be unsettling. Self-exploration is key to personal growth. By facing our inner selves and accepting who we truly are, we gain the wisdom needed to unlock life's mysteries.

Through this work, the wisdom we gain deeply affects our relationships and our environment. By embracing the power of transformation that comes from the occult, we can unlock a hidden potential and can start creating a life that we really want.

The mysteries of the occult and life's biggest questions are connected. Only through personal growth and self-discovery can we uncover the hidden knowledge at the heart of both. As we continue on this journey, let's remember that the path to understanding is guided by curiosity, self-reflection, and the honest pursuit of truth. Often, this truth requires the humility to admit things to ourselves.

Correspondence

Name: Ratziel

Hebrew: רָזִיאֵל

Color: Gray, to represent mystery.

Numerology: 2

Gematria: 248
R 200, z 7, y 10, e 1, l 30

Planet: the galaxy (all the stars)

Favored period:

Around midday and midnight, where there is no beginning or end

Avoid sunrise and sundown, which symbolizes something starting or ending

Any day of the week and month

Applications:

Revelations about yourself and the universe

Understanding philosophy

Transcendental meditation

Esoteric mysteries

Gratitude

Universal mechanics

Seeking an experience

Ratziel רָזִיאֵל

Embrace Change

Change is unavoidable. Even if it's we would try to control it, events will happen that are not planned. Keeping your heart open and your mind available to do personal growth will allow you to accept changes even if they are changes that are not planned.

Cultivate Self-Awareness

Practice observing yourself and your behavior. Self-awareness is essential so you can see yourself as you think, speak, an act. Only if you know how you are inside and how you act outside will you be available to cultivate compassion.

Seek Support

It will be difficult to do everything alone. We encourage you to seek support amongst your friends and family, even from society. In any moment you feel so lonely that you can't even bear the weight of your trials, it feels so much better to feel part of a group, even more to feel understood.

Maintain Balance

Too Much personal growth could lead to more depression. If you never do personal growth, you will never grow and you will never cultivate compassion. However if you are constantly doing personal growth, observing how you are and how you can get better, you might develop a reflex of only seeing the negative in you and never be satisfied of how you are now. Balance personal growth with personal time to enjoy yourself.

Trust the Process

It takes a lifetime to evolve into a fine being, although very early we can develop virtuous behaviors such as compassion. As you go through various life experiences, we encourage you to trust the process of evolution. The more you observe yourself, the more you grow, the more you will want to be a good person and compassion will become the natural choice for you.

The Power of Compassion

Compassion is a powerful virtue that dictates how you will act. As you cultivate compassion you will choose to act with kindness even when you are tempted to act more harshly. It is easy to act when compassion when everyone is agreeable and in harmony. The trials of compassion is especially when there is no harmony.

The more personal growth you do, the easier it will be to act with compassion; to choose a response of kindness in the face of adversity, or to do an act of charity with someone that you've judged as being too greedy. Compassion has the power to change people by giving them an example of how to act virtuously.

Tzaphkiel is the archangel that manages evolution, compassion, and the processing of experiences. It belongs in the sphere of Divine Intelligence, which is the most profound understanding of the mysteries of life, previously revealed by Ratziel. While we often associate intelligence to the understanding of academic and mechanical processes, we must here expand on the definition of Divine Intelligence, where it will encompass everything that can be understood, including personal experiences.

Tzaphkiel צַפְקִיאֵל

4- Tzadkiel צִדְקִיאֵל

Inspiration

Tzadkiel is the Archangel that brought the concept of justice to be, in our society. When humans gathered into groups and started to organize their lives together, most of us were still animal in nature. Justice is one of the rare concepts that distinguishes us from the animal world. It is where we have decided to believe in the concept of respecting each other and having a consequence when that respect is absent.

Invoking divine justice will not make you win your case in front of others. The concept of divine justice and human justice are quite different. Human justice is about how much you believe you have the rights to something. Divine justice is based on the right of every human to have an emancipated experience of life. In such, define justice will harmonize resources and opportunities for everyone equally.

Metaphysics

Inequity can be found anywhere in the world. It is one of the greatest injustices that we can find. We will find inequity amongst classes, or races, or any other group classification that allows one group to subtly oppress another.

Inequity is not only a global issue. It also happens in your immediate circle, affecting relationships among family members, friends, and coworkers. When different family members get different types of treatment; when one child seems to be the favorite at the expense of the others, or when one person in a group seems to find ways to obtain more from the activity than any other, those kind of behaviors foster irritation or even frustration, disturbing the harmony within the group. Equity is the solution to inequity, obviously.

Equity is the Best way to bring about harmony, both globally and within our smaller circles. By ensuring that everyone has an equal opportunity to the experiences they desire to live, everyone will celebrate with more joy what life can bring them.

Equity is not just about a proper distribution of, but also about everyone having access to the opportunities they hope for, and for the soul, the availability of desired experiences. The soul yearns for experiences that enrich, not only our lives, but also allow it to evolve, and equity plays a crucial role in enabling as many souls as possible to pursue the experiences they desire.

Nature distributes resources and opportunities through a process of convection and entropy. These natural mechanisms ensure that resources and energy are spread evenly throughout every ecosystem. Convection circulates heat and matter inside fluids, to maintain a stable temperatures, and bring conditions for life to flourish in. Entropy is the natural tendency for any system to move towards a state of maximum disorder or randomness, ultimately also leading to an even distribution.

By observing and understanding these natural principles, we can learn valuable lessons about achieving equity in our societies, aiming to create a more balanced and harmonious world for all. Just like nature shares resources, experiences are shared among souls too.

Nature helps things like air, water, and food to be spread out so that everything can live and grow. In the same way, souls get to have different experiences in life. Tzadkiel ensures an entropic convection of consciousness and causal energy, but that system is hindered by inequity and injustice. When everyone gets a chance to have the various experiences they desire, it's like nature's way of sharing resources. This helps us all live together in a happier and more balanced world.

Tzadkiel is the archangel of Justice, in his definition and philosophy. But Kamael, being the master of chains of events, will intercede in the fields of justice, during their resolution.

Correspondence

Name: Tzadkiel

Hebrew: צָדְקִיאֵל

Color: Blue, for justice, equity and forgiveness.

Numerology: 4

Gematria: 235
Tz 90, d 4, q 100, y 10, e 1, l 30

Planet: Jupiter

Favored period:
4am or 4pm
4rd day of the month
April, 4rd month of the year
Thursday, day of Jupiter

Applications:

Manifesting projects

Justice and equity

Forgiveness

Freedom

Detachment, letting go

Note that Tzadkiel won't help you win a cause in court, if you are guilty or in a gray zone, even if you believe yourself to be within your rights. Tzadkiel calls for Divine Justice, which is different from human justice. More philosophical training and personal growth will be useful to understand the depths of Divine Justice. Tzadkiel will come to your aid if you are clearly being abused, or subject to inequity. I, personally, would rather be guided on the path of righteousness, rather than be right about something, only for my own sake. Thankfully, both are often compatible.

Tzadkiel צַדְקִיאֵל

5- Kamael כמאֵל

Inspiration

We usually understand strength as the ability to apply force on an object, using our muscles, levers, and good method. But strength is not only a physical quality after human body. Strength is also a virtue.

Strength, as a virtue, surpasses the concept of moral strength. It is a fundamental experience based on certainty, pure trust, that gives you an unshakable confidence. Spiritual strength is behind perseverance, persistence, determination, and also that moral strength.

Strength will become either your guide, are your driving method, as you flow true a life filled with causality (cause and effect) of moving events, on the river of time. Between two calm moments of peace, good news and bad news, blessings and catastrophes alike, will show up to disturb your direction. Spiritual strength is what keeps you aiming at your goal, giving you the courage to face any trial on the way.

Metaphysics

Convection, as understood by thermodynamics, is the transfer of heat by the movement of fluids such as air or water. It can generate turbulence depending on its intensity. When the strength of convection increases, it can cause fluid to move in unpredictable ways (entropy), creating chaotic patterns of motion known as turbulence. This phenomenon is often observed in natural processes such as weather patterns or ocean currents, as well as in industrial applications such as the mixing of chemicals or the cooling of machinery. In short, the strength of convection plays a crucial role in determining the level of turbulence present in a given system.

Causality is the law of cause and effect. One event provoking the happening of another event. Often named Karma in the new age world, causality links together chains of events, not linear but more like a web. In metaphysical terms, convection is the motion of consciousness, energy and causality, as it circulates through the universe. Kamael being the archangel of strength and power, he manages that convection. We can invoke his aid regarding events that are happening because of his access to causality. The fact that he manages the convection of causality means that he won't necessarily answer a request directly, but through a series of events.

The Butterfly Effect is a concept that was introduced by meteorologist Edward Lorenz in the 1960s, which states that small changes in initial conditions can lead to significant differences in the outcome of a complex system. The name "Butterfly Effect" comes from the idea that the flap of a butterfly's wings in one part of the world can potentially cause a hurricane in another part of the world.

Occult rituals are used to influence the supernatural or spiritual realms, only to have it manifest in the physical real through an event or experience. The idea of directing the Butterfly Effect using an occult ritual suggests that one could intentionally create a small change in a system that has a significant impact on the outcome.

The idea of using an occult ritual to direct the Butterfly Effect may seem far-fetched, but it is grounded in the belief that everything in the universe is connected and that energy can be directed and manipulated through focused intention. However, it is important to note that such practices are not scientifically proven, and their efficacy may vary based on individual beliefs and practices. The Butterfly Effect is a

Kamael כמאֵל

Mikael מיכאל

7- Haniel חַנִּיאֵל

Inspiration

Haniel Constantly seen by all of us without realizing it. It is a loss of nature that ensures that every aspect of a Biome gets the opportunity it needs to grow. In human society, Haniel is the concept of charity, of caring for someone else than ourselves.

Haniel is also involved in the divine intelligence behind all phenomenon in nature. What it means for human beings, is the qualities that we have in our mind, like inspiration, creativity, intelligence in various ways. Haniel Cares about the world through a mystical form of intelligence. We, being part of nature, are dotted with that intelligence providing us with all these wonderful qualities.

Metaphysics

nature is made of a very complex and intricate web of interactions. It can be perceived as having a mind of its own, as it governs the fundamental natural laws that dictate the behavior of its various components.

One of these principles is the convection of resources. It drives the distribution and balance of vital elements throughout entire ecosystems. These natural laws are the main guiding force behind the intricate dance of life. It ensures that the systems remain in harmony as they are interconnected in a web of organisms that keep on flourishing.

Just like a human mind is shaped by instincts, emotions, and cognitive capacities, nature's mind is defined by the laws of physics, chemistry come up and biology that govern the patterns and rhythm of living beings. By understanding these natural processes we can obtain insight about the mechanics of the human being

Once more we will relate to the concept of conviction. Nature is a complex system that often employs convection to distribute resources evenly across various ecosystems. Convection is a process by which heat and matter is transported in the fluid through volumes of various properties or density. The complex movement of all of these particles create a cyclical flow.

This is where entropy comes in. It's a concept that's come from the laws of thermodynamics, measuring the degree of disorder and randomness in any given system. Entropy is the tendency for any system to move from a state of order to a state of disorder. The second law of thermodynamics states that entropy in a closed system always increases, which means that the system naturally will progress towards a more chaotic disordered state. However, overtime that chaos will evenly distribute the resources across the entire ecosystem

The relationship between convection an entropy can easily be observed and how nature distributes resources. Heating up water in a pot will cause the slowly gained temperature to evenly distribute across all of the water in that volume. In nature, we would see the humidity from the ground and lakes rise into the atmosphere under the effect of the sun, to then come back down in the form of rain. As fluids flow and circulate in convicting systems, resources a various size of particles are being transported. This chaotic dynamics helps ensure that resources are spread more evenly across the environment.

Haniel חַנִיאֵל

In the same vein, an overly rigid Cartesian mindset can prevent us from experiencing life to the fullest. Descartes' famous "Cogito, ergo sum" - "I think, therefore I am" emphasizes the importance of the mind in determining our existence. However, when taken to an extreme, this mindset leads to an unhealthy obsession with control and rationality, leaving little room for the spontaneity and vulnerability that our hearts need.

To live a truly fulfilling life, we must strike a balance between the mechanics of the mind and the heart. We need to allow ourselves to experience our emotions fully and use them as a valuable source of information to inform our intellectual understanding of the world. Likewise, we must also be willing to embrace the uncertainty and unpredictability that comes with following our hearts. This can lead to some of the most profound and meaningful experiences in our lives.

Raphael is quite mechanical, but that does not mean "obtuse cartesian intellectual". He is mechanical in the sense that he is all about the machinery that operates any and all of our systems. He will thus inspire any kind of mechanics, revealing knowledge, but also deal with matters of the heart, such as relationships. Biology is one such kind of natural knowledge, where Raphael knows all about organic systems. He will thus become, in our modern times, the angel of medicine, but also of romantic relationships, as these both concern the aspect of natural mechanics: biology.

Correspondence

Name: Raphael

Hebrew: רְפָאל

Color: Orange

Numerology: 8

Gematria: 311
R 200, ph 80, e 1, l 30

Planet: Mercury

Favored period:

During the day for intellectual matters

After sundown for matters of the heart

8am or 8pm, for any request

8th day of the month

August, 8th month of the year

Wednesday, day of Mercury

Applications:

Understanding, learning

Psychology

Medicine, health

Romance, human relationships

Raphael רָפָאל

9- Gabriel גַבְרִיאֵל

Inspiration

Gabriel, often known as the messenger of God, is a misunderstanding of its true nature. Gabriel being the closest to the physical plane, makes it much easier to perceive by physical beings. Thus, it was seen as a messenger, for it was easier to see or hear.

Gabriel is in fact the Strength of God, much differently than would be Kamael. Gabriel is in the 9th sephiroth, the plane of life, will, and energy. Gabriel makes us strong, physically. He provides energy and willpower. It is also the archangel that links the mind and the body.

Metaphysics

Albeit this book covers the esoteric and occult aspects of angelology and rituals, let's delve into the fascinating difference between the ethereal and manifest material worlds, exploring the intricate interplay between quantum physics, quantum geometry, and the human mind. Our quest to comprehend these seemingly disparate realms will reveal how the power of human will and consciousness may bridge the gap between the ethereal and material worlds.

While many ancient texts have covered the subject, I wish here to use subjective references to the newest scientific theories on the matter, hoping to inspire the mind of our generation. If the this short theorical text seems to steep to understand, you may skip to the next sub-section: The Will to Manifest.

The manifest material world we perceive and interact with daily is characterized by objects with mass, occupying space and exhibiting various densities. Density, in this context, refers to the amount of mass per unit volume. In contrast, the ethereal world is often described as an intangible realm, devoid of conventional physical attributes, and is more closely linked to the domain of consciousness and energy.

Quantum physics provides a framework that may help explain the relationship between the ethereal and material worlds. At its core, quantum mechanics acknowledges that particles, such as electrons, can exhibit both wave-like and particle-like behavior. This wave-particle duality suggests that particles are not confined to a single location, but exist in a superposition of states until they are observed. This concept is exemplified by the famous double-slit experiment, which demonstrates that particles can interfere with themselves as if they were waves, even when they are not being observed. We spare you, here, the long explanation about this double-slit experiment, but invite you to search on it, if you are curious.

The ethereal world may be thought of as a realm where particles exist in their uncollapsed, wave-like state, representing an infinite array of potential outcomes. In contrast, the material world represents the manifestation of a single outcome, resulting from the collapse of these wave functions through observation or interaction.

Quantum geometry, an area of study in theoretical physics, seeks to describe the fundamental structure of space and time at the smallest possible scales. In this framework, space and time are considered quantized, meaning they exist in discrete units rather than being continuous. These units, known as Planck lengths and Planck times, represent the smallest possible divisions of space and time.

Quantum geometry suggests that the fabric of reality is woven from these quantized building blocks, with both the ethereal and material worlds being different expressions of this fundamental structure. The ethereal world may represent the unmanifested potential of this fabric, while the material world represents the manifested, observable reality.

The power of the human mind and will are essential in understanding the relationship between the ethereal and material worlds. As conscious beings, our thoughts, intentions, and actions shape our reality, influencing the potential outcomes represented by the ethereal world's quantum wave functions.

By focusing our minds and channeling our willpower, we may be able to affect the probabilities of these outcomes, effectively "breaching the veil" between the ethereal and material worlds. This concept has been explored in various contexts, such as the observer effect in quantum mechanics and the study of psi phenomena, including telekinesis and remote viewing.

Ultimately, our understanding of the ethereal and material worlds, and the relationship between them, is still in its infancy. However, the emerging connections between quantum physics, quantum geometry, and human consciousness promise to reveal a deeper understanding of reality and the power we have to shape it.

The Will to Manifest

Let us here express in a more esoteric dialect the premises explained in the above. Throughout the ages, human beings have sought to manifest their desires and turn their dreams into reality. While countless methods and practices exist to accomplish this, one particular approach has remained shrouded in mystery and intrigue – the use of occult rituals. By harnessing the potent forces of emotional desire and willpower, these rituals amplify the manifestation process, allowing practitioners to achieve their goals and fulfill their deepest aspirations.

Central to the manifestation process is the integration of one's emotional desires and willpower. Emotions serve as a catalyst, igniting the power of the mind and the passion to pursue one's objectives. Emotions also amplify and orient our will. Willpower, on the other hand, is the driving force that propels an individual to stay focused and committed to their goals, despite any obstacles that may arise. Willpower densifies thoughts and emotions and projects them into the manifest world.

Occult rituals have long been utilized as a tool for amplifying this process. Through the use of symbolism, ceremony, and intention, practitioners are able to access the hidden realms of consciousness, summoning the help of external agent like angels, tapping into the potent energies that lie just beyond the veil of everyday reality. By engaging with these esoteric practices, one can amplify the powers of emotion and will, resulting in an accelerated manifestation process.

Gabriel is the angel responsible for this transition between the ethereal and manifest world. This is why Gabriel is often the angel seen when a Judeo-Christian person receives a revelation. Gabriel was called The Messenger for this reason, however not for his communications skills, but for his innate ability to densify himself enough for humans to perceive her.

Gabriel גַבְרִיאֵל

In the realm of mythology and angelology, the figure of Sandalphon stands tall, an angelic being with profound influence over the natural order of the universe. Tasked with the monumental responsibility of overseeing the laws of physics and chemistry, Sandalphon is the celestial architect of the manifest world, ensuring the stability and harmony of the cosmos.

As the divine force responsible for the precise balance of the universe, Sandalphon's presence permeates the very fabric of existence. From the macroscopic scale of celestial bodies to the microscopic realm of atomic particles, the angel's meticulous guidance is felt. It is through Sandalphon's wisdom and tireless effort that the world operates, and life thrives.

The role of Sandalphon in managing the laws of physics is nothing short of miraculous. By maintaining the delicate balance of fundamental forces - gravity, electromagnetism, the strong nuclear force, and the weak nuclear force - the celestial architect guarantees the stability and predictability of the cosmos. Through these forces, matter and energy interact and transform, giving rise to the intricate dance of the universe both in manifest and ethereal form.

In addition to the laws of physics, Sandalphon also presides over the realm of chemistry, ensuring the interactions between atoms and molecules unfold as intended. The angel's influence extends to the formation and breaking of chemical bonds, enabling the construction of complex molecules essential for life. Through Sandalphon's guidance, elements come together, creating the diverse building blocks that constitute our world.

But even amidst the ordered beauty of the universe, chaos and entropy persist. Some may wonder if the presence of such disorder is a flaw in Sandalphon's celestial design. However, the divine wisdom of the angel ensures that entropy serves a vital purpose: it fuels the ongoing evolution and transformation of the cosmos, driving change and renewal.

In human culture, Sandalphon is often depicted as a radiant figure, surrounded by the symbols of the natural world. The reverence for this celestial architect is a testament to the deep connection between humanity and the universe. By contemplating the works of Sandalphon, we are reminded of the complex interplay of forces that make life possible and the divine beauty that lies within the order and chaos of the cosmos.

In conclusion, the angel Sandalphon, as the celestial architect of the universe, plays an essential role in maintaining the delicate balance of the laws of physics and chemistry. Through this divine guidance, the cosmos operates harmoniously, providing a stable foundation for life to flourish. It is in the understanding and appreciation of Sandalphon's role that we may find inspiration and awe in the miraculous beauty of our world.

Ezekiel 1:15-6 "As I watched the four creatures, I saw something that looked like a wheel on the ground beside each of the four-faced creatures. This is what the wheels looked like: They were identical wheels, sparkling like diamonds in the sun. It looked like they were wheels within wheels, like a gyroscope."

The wheels referred to by Ezekiel is the Power and Wizdom of Sandalphon. It is the entropic convection resulting from the four forces of physics and the laws of chemistry. Analyzing each letter of his name, Sandalphon means "natural forces invested and transmitted to every other part of nature". For the harmony that he presides, he was called the Angel of Music, for his role managing a symbolic orchestra of natural forces.

Correspondence

Name: Sandalphon

Hebrew: סַנְדַּלְפוֹן

Color: Brown, olive, brick red, dark yellow, earth colors.

Numerology: 10

Gematria: 930
S 60, n 50, d 4, l 30, ph 80, v 6, n 700

Planet: Earth

Favored period:
Any time of day
1st, 10th, 20th and 30th of the month

Applications:
Manifesting
Having a place, or home
Having a purpose
Organising, orchestrating
Physical health
Communication
Music
Simplicity
Reality

Sandalphon סַנְדַּלְפוֹן

Exhaustive list of application

Here we wish to provide a more exhaustive list of applications for each archangel, as it was understood or interpreted by modern occultists and new-agers. You will see that many applications can be found across many archangels. The deeper we go in this list, the more we'll realize that we can ask just about anything to any archangel, and they will use their specific field of influence to help us achieve our objectives. A more profound understanding of each archangel will help us orient our choices when we define our ritual.

Metatron

Archangel Metatron is often associated with sacred geometry, divine knowledge, and spiritual growth. Here are some of the ways in which Metatron is used in rituals and prayers:

Protection: Metatron is often called upon for protection against negative energies and entities.

Guidance: Metatron is believed to provide guidance and support on spiritual journeys, helping individuals to connect with their higher selves and align with their soul's purpose.

Manifestation: Metatron is associated with the manifestation of desires and intentions, and can be called upon to assist in manifesting abundance, love, and other blessings.

Healing: Metatron is often called upon for healing of physical, emotional, and spiritual ailments. He is believed to work through the chakras and energy centers to promote balance and harmony.

Meditation: Metatron is often used as a focal point in meditation, particularly in practices that involve visualizing sacred geometry.

Communication: Metatron is considered a powerful communicator and is often called upon to help individuals communicate more effectively, both with others and with the divine.

Activating Higher Consciousness: Metatron is believed to help individuals activate higher levels of consciousness and access spiritual insights and wisdom.

Forgiveness: Metatron is believed to help individuals release old patterns and negative emotions, allowing them to forgive themselves and others and move forward in a more positive and productive way.

Ascension: Metatron is often called upon to assist individuals on their journey of ascension, helping them to raise their vibration and align with higher levels of consciousness.

Prayer: Many people include Metatron in their daily prayers, asking for guidance, protection, healing, and other blessings.

8- Raphael רְפָאל

Inspiration

Rafael. is the archangel of all forms of understanding. We should start by distinguishing various kinds of intelligences, such as practical intelligence, emotional intelligence, and academic intelligence, which will all later expand into spiritual intelligence.

Strange in our society, to place the concept of Understanding at the emotional level, the mechanical sephirah of Hod. Before education was well spread, in the last 100 years or so, academic education was scarce. Most humans, since the beginning of the Homo Sapiens, never went to school, never learned to read or write. Most leaned to count only at the mental and verbal level. Hence, in a world mostly non-academic, the concept of Understanding was attributed to having enough experience with something so that it would make sense.

In that way, Raphael is the archangel of all forms of understanding. True understanding comes from feeling a concept or an experience. Even while studying hard mathematical concepts, when we finally grasp it, we feel a "joy of understanding", a feeling of "Eureka, I got it". A realization, even at the intellectual level, is both a mental and emotional experience.

Thus Raphael can be the master of knowledge, and relationship. It is the emotional-mental activities that work together in unison, to encompass all kinds of knowledge and relationship.

Metaphysics

The archangel Raphael is all about the mind, knowledge, mechanics… yet he is situated in the sphere of Hod, and the emotional plane. Why is that? In our society, we have a very limited understanding of the mind, where we tend to make a clear scission between the intellectual and emotional aspects of the mind. Whereas, the intellect and the heart are actually one and the same, with both a cartesian and chaotic aspect.

It is often said that the mind and the heart are two sides of the same coin. As humans, we have developed intricate systems to govern our thoughts, emotions, and behavior. Our minds are like well-oiled machines, working tirelessly to process, analyze and make sense of the world around us. As for our hearts, they are in sync with our emotions and desires. These two complex systems work hand in hand, ensuring a harmonious balance that allows us to live fulfilling lives.

The mechanics of the mind and heart are deeply intertwined. One cannot function optimally without the other. The mind's intellectual understanding of the world helps us navigate our experiences, while the heart's emotional intelligence enables us to process our feelings and form meaningful connections with others.

When we repress our emotions or deny our experiences, we inadvertently limit our intellectual understanding of the world. Emotions are an integral part of the human experience, and by suppressing them, we cut ourselves off from a vital source of information. Emotional intelligence is just as important as cognitive intelligence. Denying ourselves the opportunity to feel and understand our emotions hinders our ability to make sense of our experiences and the world around us, and build pressure inside, that will eventually need to come out.

Inspiration

Tzaphkiel is a great concept of compassion that pervades the entire universe. Tzaphkiel is the power that teams the great transformation that the universe is going through as it creates and forms itself. It's power tampers the friction of all the energies intertwined in the moment of the creation, and as the universe keeps transforming itself.

The intensity of that turbulence is so powerful that it would destroy the things that it is trying to create if it was not tampered with another kind of energy that softens, lubricates, and harmonizes all these moving parts. Tzaphkiel Comes to sue them the process so we can have enough time to process each experience as we go through them.

Imagine if you would go through a heartbreak, then 15 minutes later got fired from your job, then receive a great gift, for only an hour or so later learned that a parent has died, but that your cousin just gave birth... giving you no time to process any of these experiences. It would be impossible to survive if every few minutes of our lives we would have one of those dramatic life changing moments.

Compassion contains this deep understanding of evolution as it allows us to soothe and dampen the blows, giving us time to process each of these experiences, so we can heal what was hurt and rejoice for what is to be celebrated.

Metaphysics

In life, the sum of our experiences comes together to shape who we are. Each experience will contribute to who we are, what we become. Through these experiences we learn, evolve, grow. These experiences are necessary for us to progress in our journey. However, too many strong experiences in a short time can bring destruction rather than transformation.

Divine revelations or sudden moments of insight can speed up personal growth. These revelations often bring clarity and purpose and can come from anything. A book, a conversation, quiet reflection, or sometimes even a dream. Usually, they are triggered by life experiences, whether big or small.

The two concepts of transformation and destruction, both refer to a change. They signify a new state of things, that is different form the state before. Therefor the difference between transformation and destruction, is whether that change is beneficial overall, and a hindrance.

Each change we go through requires a bit of adaptation. These changes also tire us, which requires us to rest and heal from a great event that transformed us. Having too many changes at the same time will tax our body and mind, causing pressure, and ultimately disease.

The best way to promote positive transformation and avoid destruction is to approach personal growth with patience and determination. By recognizing when change is happening too fast, we can take measures to soften the blows, and slow down the process, which will ensure that our journey remains constructive.

Correspondence

Name: Tzaphkiel

Hebrew: צָפְקִיאֵל

Color: Indigo, dark blue, representing deep spirituality.

Numerology: 3

Gematria: 311
Tz 90, ph 80, q 100, y 10, e 1, l 30

Planet: Saturn

Favored period:

3pm for birth, or coming in the world

3am for death, departing from the world

Any hour for any other related topic

3rd day of the month

March, 3rd month of the year

Saturday, day of Saturn

Applications:

Personal growth

Religious and spiritual matters

Funeral rites, birth, life and death

Cultivation of virtues (mainly Compassion)

Divine intelligence

Compassion

Transformation

fascinating concept that suggests even small actions can have significant impacts on complex systems, such as chains of causality.

Any attempt to directly control the world through the use of occult rituals is likely to have disastrous karmic implications. The idea of manipulating energy and influencing the supernatural realm is often associated with the belief in karma, which suggests that every action has a consequence. When attempting to exert control over the natural order of the universe, one risks disrupting the delicate balance of cause and effect, which can lead to negative consequences. Moreover, attempting to control the world through occult rituals may be seen as an act of arrogance and can result in a buildup of negative karma. Therefore, it is essential to approach such practices with respect and caution and to consider the potential consequences of one's actions.

That is why, with a ritual to Kamal, we are asking Him to manage the causal webs, from a place of humility and detachment. Let us use a metaphor to better explain ourselves. When it comes to tasks that require (a universal scale) expertise, it is often better to seek the help of a professional rather than attempting to do it ourselves. Professionals have the necessary knowledge and experience to complete tasks quickly and efficiently, while also ensuring that the final outcome meets high standards. Moreover, by enlisting the help of a professional, we can avoid making costly (karmic) mistakes that could potentially result in more significant problems down the line.

We must admit that we certainly don't have the level of competence, as a mere human, to understand the enormous amount of ramifications in the flow of causality. We shall do rituals to Kamael, so that He will operate the butterfly effect, while respecting the universal balance of all things.

Kamael would therefore apply to the field of justice, being intimately involved with causality. While the true nature of Divine Justice is associated to Tzadkiel, for it directly relates to equity, Kamael will often be invoked in trials of justice, asking him to make the outcome favorable to us, and hopefully alleviate the intensity of turbulence. However, keep in mind that no archangel will declare you innocent if you have caused an imbalance in the ebb and flow of causality. Archangels bring about Divine Justice, not justification.

We should not confuse Kamael (first letter Kaph) with Chamuel (first letter Hret), who's fields of application would include love and relationships, which topics we decided to cover various aspects in the chapters of Mikael, Haniel and Raphael.

6- Mikael מיכאל

Inspiration

Our survival instinct makes us want to satisfy our physical needs before anything else. Once our needs are met, that survival instinct keeps pushing it into satisfying our physical desires. That leads to materialism that comes with a load of negative side effects. A spiritual quest, pondering metaphysical concepts, philosophising and contemplating the unseen, is the way to alleviate the troubles brought by materialism.

Mikael will help us on our spiritual quest. He will guide us in developing virtuous behaviors, empathy, understanding at all levels.

Metaphysics

Materialism is ever present in our lives. It is the main motivations that influences our decisions. Before judging it as a sin, let's consider our instinct of survival. Before we can care for spiritual pondering, we have to ensure that we are fed, protected from the elements, and have a comfortable place to sleep. It is totally natural for anyone to want health and comfort before delving on the philosophical path.

However, this instinct of satisfying our physical needs persists once we have health and comfort, to the point that it becomes an obsession to acquire and accumulate physical goods beyond a healthy point. Materialism then brings about its own series of difficulties and problems, both physical and mental.

The name "Mikael" translates as "Who is (like) God?". It's not a name, it's a question. It's an invitation to start pondering on philosophical and spiritual concepts that would better our life. It is the beginning of a serious mystical endeavor, aiming at resolving the complications deriving from materialistic behavior.

The name "Mikael" has deep roots in various religious and spiritual traditions. Its Hebrew origin, מיכאל (Mīkā'ēl), is composed of two parts: "Mi" meaning "who" and "ka" meaning "like," together with "El," which refers to God. "Who is like God?", for the agnostic, would be "What is Divine?".

Materialism is the excessive focus on material possessions and wealth. While it seems to be prevalent in modern society, it actually was always present throughout history. Materialism will lead to a decreased satisfaction with everything life has to offer. It puts a strain on relationships. It increases mental health issues, and has a negative effect on the environment. In this age, and very mental degradation is a concern more present than in the past.

As we keep on pursuing material success at all costs, it leaves us with little room for spiritual exploration and personal growth. And while the negative effects pile up, we try to answer the problems with even more materialistic solutions. Again, all motivated by our survival instinct, when driven overboard.

Spiritual pondering, while not obvious, is the antidote to materialism and its side effects. Asking ourselves spiritual questions, as motivated by the name Mikhail, Will bring about a broader perspective on life. Fostering a sense of gratitude and contentment, will alleviates the materialistic impulse. Cultivating inner peace will bring more resilience towards the various trials of life. A spiritual attitude also deepens our connection with others and the world, bringing about harmony for everyone.

remain grounded. Without gravity, the Earth would dissolve into the void, and life, as we know it, would cease to exist.

Electromagnetism, responsible for the interaction between charged particles, also plays a vital role in the chaotic entropic patterns. The interplay of electric and magnetic fields creates a complex tapestry of forces that guide the behavior of matter, from the smallest atomic particles to the largest technological marvels.

The strong nuclear force and the weak nuclear force complete the ensemble. The strong force binds protons and neutrons together in the atomic nucleus, while the weak force governs the radioactive decay of subatomic particles. These forces work behind the scenes, enabling atoms to bond, forming the myriad of molecules that make up our world.

Entropy is the invisible hand that directs this cosmic dance. As the laws of physics push and pull matter, energy is continually redistributed within the system. Entropy increases over time, transforming ordered energy into disordered energy, fueling the perpetual march of chaos.

On Earth, these entropic patterns can be observed everywhere – in the swirling of gases in the atmosphere, the crashing of waves upon the shore, and the growth and decay of living organisms. The laws of physics, working in harmony with entropy, give rise to a mesmerizing symphony of chaos and order.

The chaotic entropic patterns formed by the interplay of the laws of physics create a vibrant, ever-changing tapestry of life on Earth. It is through the understanding of these patterns and the forces that shape them that we gain a deeper appreciation for the beauty and complexity of our world.

Inspiration

Sandalphon is described by Ezekiel as '"The wheels within the wheels"'. This refers to the mechanics of fluids, such as convection and turbulence. Sandalphon is the archangelic expression of the laws of physics. He resides in the 10th sephiroth of Malkut, the physical plane. He is a densification at the physical level of the mechanics of consciousness that operates on all planes.

Sandalphon is all about mass, the world, the body, and the intricate laws of nature. He will help you ground yourself and see the spiritual nature of the physical world. He will help you manifest, organize without control, follow the flow without getting lost.

Metaphysics

In the realm of physics, a wondrous dance of matter takes place, governed by the intricate choreography of fundamental forces. The laws of nature are like the strings of a puppeteer, dictating the push and pull of matter, driving the never-ending performance of the universe. Entropy, a measure of the chaos and disorder within a system, reigns supreme as the director of this cosmic ballet.

Our Earth, a blue-green gem in the vastness of space, is no exception to this rule. Within its depths, on its surface, and in the atmosphere above, matter interacts, driven by the laws of physics, forging chaotic entropic patterns.

Gravity, the force of attraction between objects with mass, is a key player in the dance. It governs the motions of celestial bodies and ensures that objects on Earth

Correspondence

Name: Kamael

Hebrew: כמאֶל

Color: Red, for strength and energy.

Numerology: 5

Gematria: 91
K 20, m 40, e 1, 1 30

Planet: Mars

Favored period:
Sunrise to activate causality
Sundown to calm turbulence
5rd day of the month
May, 5rd month of the year
Tuesday, day of Mars

Applications:
Life force, energy
Determination, perseverance, courage
Empowering a project
Managing turbulence, tolerance
Causality, justice
Spiritual influence, causality
Moral strength

In the animal Kingdom, we can observe many wild species exhibit a cooperative behavior that promote the equitable distribution of food amongst the members have a group. Meaning that even sentient being will tend to have a behavior that follows the laws of convection an entropy. Social dynamics will often rise and animals living in groups, such as wolves, meerkats and primates, Where individuals work together when they hunt or forage. This cooperation benefits the entire group by maximizing everyone's chance at survival an opportunities for reproduction.

Although humans possess the capacity for cooperation an altruism, they also possess the flaws of greed, Which is a trait that can hinder the natural process of sharing resource in an equitable fashion. Greed, the desire for excessive material wealth, power, or even status, contributes to iniquity, an unbalanced distribution of the resources. To resolve this challenge, it is important for societies to promote values and that emphasise compassion and empathy.

In order to cultivate a good relationship with Haniel, we must thrive to deepen our sense of equity through charity. We should do so without becoming the savior of the world, hindering our own emancipation for others to have it. We must find a balance that suits us, in how much we share, and how much we want for ourselves. Taking care of our own need is not narcissistic, it is actually a form of self-love.

When a society emancipates itself, when the majority of its members feel a certain sense of satisfaction, their mind can dwell on intellectual, philosophical and artistic matters. Our intellect thrives better when our body is not fighting with its basic needs. Haniel is the archangel of intelligence, art, philosophy, creativity, and nature. He is the symbol of an emancipated mind.

Correspondence

Name: Haniel

Hebrew: חַנִּיאֵל

Color: Green, for nature and charity

Numerology: 7

Gematria: 99
Hr 8, n 50, I 10, e 1, l 30

Planet: Venus

Favored period:
During the day for intellectual matters, after sundown for matters of nature
7am or 7pm, for any request
7th day of the month
July, 7th month of the year
Friday, day of Venus

Applications:
Intellectual and artistic emancipation
Relationship with nature
Mental health
Extra-sensory perception
Creativity
Charity

Correspondence

Name: Gabriel

Hebrew: גַבְרִיאֵל

Color: Purple

Numerology: 9

Gematria: 246
G 3, b 2, r 200, I 10, e 1, l 30

Planet: Moon

Favored period:
9am or 9pm, for any request
9th, 18th and 27th day of the month
September, 9th month of the year
Monday, day of the Moon

Applications:

- New moon: sleeping, resting, clearing the mind, new beginnings

- Waxing Crescent: initiating a project, awakening phase

- First Quarter: gathering resources

- Waxing Gibbous: planning, organising everything before an event

- Full moon: manifesting, have space, being present, productivity

- Waning Gibbous: reaping benefits

- Third Quarter: rejoicing, enjoying life
- Waning Crescent: preparing for sleep or rest, retirement

The moon being so influential in every esoteric tradition, we feel we should explain more the types of applications, that you can use anytime, or in conjunction with the phases of the moon, or combining with other planet influences, if it is easy to add this extra correspondence in the making of your ritual.

In astrology, the moon moves through the 12 zodiac signs approximately every 28 days, and the sign it's in at a given time can affect how a person feels and behaves. If you perform your ritual while the moon is in your birth or ascendant sign, even better. But you should not limit yourself or delay your ritual for this minor influence. You can search online for "in which astrological sign is the moon now".

The moon is associated with emotions, feelings, intuition, and the subconscious mind. It is said to govern the mother-child relationship, nurturing, and caretaking instincts. The full moon is thought to be a time of heightened emotions and energy, while the new moon is seen as a time of new beginnings and fresh starts.

The moon's influence is said to be strongest in the astrological sign it is currently transiting through, with different signs having different effects on emotions and behaviors. Astrology is not at all the focus of this book, and you should only consider the minor influence of planets if you are skilled in astrology.

Correspondence

Name: Mikael

Hebrew: מיכאל

Color: Golden, yellow, for wisdom and light.

Numerology: 6

Gematria: 101
M 40, I 10, k 20, e 1, l 30

Planet: Sun

Favored period:
Sunrise for revelations, awakening
Sunset for personal growth and introspection
6am or 6pm, for any request
6th day of the month
June, 6th month of the year
Sunday, day of the Sun

Applications:
Wisdom, personal growth
Understanding
Liberation from suffering
Building good relationships
Protection from negativity
Faith, relationship with God

There are many ways to embrace spirituality in our lives. Let's consider a few strategies to help us in that endeavor. We can set aside time for meditation, prayer, and quiet reflections. We can engage in meaningful conversations about spirituality with those who are interested; it usually isn't productive with those who are not interested, and we should respect them.

Reading spiritual texts, and attending various workshops to expand our understanding of the spiritual path, is a great way to deep in our spiritual experience. We can also consider volunteering a bit of our time and resources to help others, giving back to society, only to cultivate this sense of gratitude and usefulness.

The main purpose of Mikael, therefore, is the revelation of the "Dharma", the embracing and understanding of life experiences in order to extract profound wisdom. Whatever you will ask Mikael, he will answer by pushing you towards the enlightenment required to answer your plea.

Raziel

Archangel Raziel is known as the "keeper of secrets" and is associated with esoteric knowledge and divine wisdom. Here are some of the ways in which Raziel is used in rituals and prayers:

Insight and Wisdom: Raziel is often called upon for insights and wisdom, helping individuals to gain deeper understanding of spiritual truths and their own path in life.

Manifestation: Raziel is associated with manifestation and can be called upon to assist in manifesting one's desires and intentions.

Healing: Raziel is believed to have healing powers and can be called upon for physical, emotional, and spiritual healing.

Protection: Raziel is often called upon for protection against negative energies and entities.

Dream Interpretation: Raziel is believed to assist in interpreting dreams and understanding their deeper meaning.

Divination: Raziel can be called upon for divination and accessing higher realms of consciousness.

Inspiration: Raziel is known for providing inspiration and creative ideas, particularly for artistic and spiritual endeavors.

Higher Consciousness: Raziel is often called upon to assist individuals in raising their consciousness and connecting with higher realms of existence.

Spiritual Growth: Raziel is associated with spiritual growth and can be called upon to assist in personal and spiritual development.

Prayer: Many people include Raziel in their daily prayers, asking for insights, guidance, protection, and blessings.

Tzaphkiel

Archangel Tzaphkiel is known as the "angel of contemplation" and is associated with spiritual transformation, inner wisdom, and self-reflection. Here are some of the ways in which Tzaphkiel is used in rituals and prayers:

Meditation: Tzaphkiel is often called upon in meditation practices to assist in quieting the mind and connecting with one's inner self.

Spiritual Insight: Tzaphkiel is believed to provide spiritual insight and can be called upon for guidance in personal and spiritual matters.

Transformation: Tzaphkiel is associated with transformation and can be called upon to assist in letting go of old patterns and embracing new ones.

Healing: Tzaphkiel is believed to have healing powers and can be called upon for physical, emotional, and spiritual healing.

Divine Connection: Tzaphkiel is associated with connecting with the divine and can be called upon to help individuals deepen their spiritual practices.

Forgiveness: Tzaphkiel is known for helping individuals release negative emotions and patterns, allowing for forgiveness and moving forward in a positive direction.

Higher Consciousness: Tzaphkiel is often called upon to assist individuals in raising their consciousness and connecting with higher realms of existence.

Self-Reflection: Tzaphkiel is associated with self-reflection and can be called upon to assist in developing a deeper understanding of oneself.

Prayer: Many people include Tzaphkiel in their daily prayers, asking for guidance, protection, healing, and blessings.

Spiritual Growth: Tzaphkiel is associated with spiritual growth and can be called upon to assist in personal and spiritual development.

Tzadkiel

Archangel Tzadkiel is known as the "angel of mercy" and is associated with forgiveness, compassion, and spiritual growth. Here are some of the ways in which Tzadkiel is used in rituals and prayers:

Forgiveness: Tzadkiel is often called upon for assistance in forgiving oneself and others, and for releasing negative emotions.

Compassion: Tzadkiel is associated with compassion and can be called upon to assist in developing a more compassionate heart and attitude towards others.

Spiritual Growth: Tzadkiel is often called upon to assist in spiritual growth, helping individuals to deepen their spiritual practices and understandings.

Healing: Tzadkiel is believed to have healing powers and can be called upon for physical, emotional, and spiritual healing.

Protection: Tzadkiel is often called upon for protection against negative energies and entities.

Divine Guidance: Tzadkiel is associated with divine guidance and can be called upon for assistance in making decisions and finding one's path in life.

Purification: Tzadkiel is believed to assist in purifying the mind, body, and spirit.

Gratitude: Tzadkiel is often called upon for assistance in cultivating gratitude and appreciation for the blessings in one's life.

Prayer: Many people include Tzadkiel in their daily prayers, asking for guidance, protection, healing, and blessings.

Intercession: Tzadkiel is believed to intercede on behalf of individuals, helping to bring about positive outcomes and blessings in their lives.

Kamael

Archangel Kamael is known as the "angel of courage" and is associated with strength, protection, and justice. Here are some of the ways in which Kamael is used in rituals and prayers:

Protection: Kamael is often called upon for protection against negative energies and entities.

Strength: Kamael is associated with strength and can be called upon for assistance in facing challenges and overcoming obstacles.

Justice: Kamael is associated with justice and can be called upon to assist in bringing about fair and equitable outcomes.

Spiritual Growth: Kamael is often called upon to assist in spiritual growth, helping individuals to develop a stronger connection with the divine and deepen their spiritual practices.

Healing: Kamael is believed to have healing powers and can be called upon for physical, emotional, and spiritual healing.

Courage: Kamael is known for assisting individuals in developing courage, particularly in situations where it may be difficult to stand up for oneself or others.

Divine Will: Kamael is associated with the divine will and can be called upon for assistance in aligning oneself with one's true purpose and path.

Leadership: Kamael is often called upon for assistance in developing leadership skills and qualities.

Prayer: Many people include Kamael in their daily prayers, asking for guidance, protection, healing, and blessings.

Overcoming Fear: Kamael is believed to assist individuals in overcoming fear and anxiety, allowing them to move forward with greater confidence and clarity.

Mikael

While Archangel Mikael is clearly defined in occult science as the archangel of wisdom and spiritual experiences, he is known in modern times as the "angel of protection" and is associated with courage, strength, and divine guidance. When he intercedes in any field of these modern fields, he will do so via his true nature, which is awakening us to a higher wisdom, often facilitating personal growth. We could say, metaphorically, that you are protected from falling in to the pit by the wisdom of seeing the pit.

Here are some of the ways in which Mikael is used in rituals and prayers:

Protection: Mikael is often called upon for protection against negative energies and entities.

Courage: Mikael is associated with courage and can be called upon for assistance in facing challenges and overcoming fear.

Strength: Mikael is known for providing strength, particularly during times of difficulty or crisis.

Divine Guidance: Mikael is often called upon for guidance, particularly in matters of spiritual growth and personal development.

Healing: Mikael is believed to have healing powers and can be called upon for physical, emotional, and spiritual healing.

Justice: Mikael is associated with justice and can be called upon to assist in bringing about fair and equitable outcomes.

Divine Will: Mikael is known for assisting individuals in aligning themselves with the divine will and purpose.

Protection of Relationships: Mikael is often called upon to protect and strengthen relationships, particularly romantic partnerships.

Prayer: Many people include Mikael in their daily prayers, asking for guidance, protection, healing, and blessings.

Overcoming Negative Habits and Addictions: Mikael is believed to assist individuals in overcoming negative habits and addictions, allowing them to lead a more fulfilling and purposeful life.

Haniel

Archangel Haniel is known as the "angel of grace" and is associated with beauty, harmony, and spiritual illumination. Here are some of the ways in which Haniel is used in rituals and prayers:

Beauty and Harmony: Haniel is often called upon for assistance in finding and creating beauty and harmony in one's life.

Spiritual Illumination: Haniel is associated with spiritual illumination and can be called upon for assistance in deepening one's spiritual practices and understanding.

Emotional Healing: Haniel is believed to have healing powers and can be called upon for emotional healing and support.

Divine Guidance: Haniel is often called upon for guidance, particularly in matters related to spiritual growth and personal development.

Relationship Healing: Haniel is associated with healing and strengthening relationships, particularly romantic partnerships.

Lunar Magic: While associated to the planet Vesus, Haniel is often associated with lunar magic and can be called upon for assistance in working with the energy of the moon.

Intuition: Haniel is known for enhancing intuition and can be called upon to assist in developing one's psychic abilities.

Forgiveness: Haniel is often called upon for assistance in forgiveness, particularly in letting go of past hurts and resentments.

Prayer: Many people include Haniel in their daily prayers, asking for guidance, protection, healing, and blessings.

Self-Expression: Haniel is associated with self-expression and can be called upon to assist in developing one's creative abilities and finding one's voice.

Raphael

Archangel Raphael is known as the "angel of healing" and is associated with physical, emotional, and spiritual healing. Here are some of the ways in which Raphael is used in rituals and prayers:

Physical Healing: Raphael is often called upon for physical healing, particularly for illnesses and injuries.

Emotional Healing: Raphael is associated with emotional healing and can be called upon for support in releasing emotional pain and trauma.

Spiritual Healing: Raphael is believed to have the ability to heal on a spiritual level, helping individuals to connect with their higher selves and find inner peace.

Divine Guidance: Raphael is often called upon for guidance, particularly in matters related to health and well-being.

Protection: Raphael is known for providing protection, particularly for those who are undergoing healing processes.

Relationship Healing: Raphael is often called upon for assistance in healing and strengthening relationships, particularly romantic partnerships.

Intercession: Raphael is believed to intercede on behalf of individuals, helping to bring about positive outcomes and blessings in their lives.

Prayer: Many people include Raphael in their daily prayers, asking for guidance, healing, and blessings.

Purification: Raphael is associated with purification and can be called upon to assist in releasing negative energy and promoting spiritual growth.

Spiritual Development: Raphael is often called upon to assist in spiritual development, helping individuals to deepen their connection with the divine and understand their true purpose in life.

Gabriel

Archangel Gabriel is known as the "messenger of God" and is associated with communication, creativity, and guidance. Here are some of the ways in which Gabriel is used in rituals and prayers:

Communication: Gabriel is often called upon for assistance in communication, particularly in expressing oneself with clarity and grace.

Creativity: Gabriel is associated with creativity and can be called upon for assistance in developing artistic abilities and finding inspiration.

Guidance: Gabriel is often called upon for guidance, particularly in matters related to personal and spiritual growth.

Spiritual Growth: Gabriel is known for assisting individuals in their spiritual growth, helping them to deepen their connection with the divine.

Prophecy: Gabriel is often associated with prophecy and can be called upon for assistance in developing prophetic abilities.

Protection: Gabriel is known for providing protection, particularly for those who are undergoing spiritual and creative processes.

Intercession: Gabriel is believed to intercede on behalf of individuals, helping to bring about positive outcomes and blessings in their lives.

Pregnancy and Childbirth: Gabriel is often called upon for assistance in pregnancy and childbirth, particularly for protection and guidance.

Prayer: Many people include Gabriel in their daily prayers, asking for guidance, inspiration, and blessings.

Manifestation: Gabriel is associated with manifestation and can be called upon to assist in manifesting one's desires and intentions.

Sandalphon

Archangel Sandalphon is known as the "angel of music" and is associated with prayer, manifestation, and communication. Here are some of the ways in which Sandalphon is used in rituals and prayers:

Prayer: Sandalphon is often called upon for assistance in prayer, helping individuals to connect with the divine and receive guidance and blessings.

Manifestation: Sandalphon is associated with manifestation and can be called upon to assist in manifesting one's desires and intentions.

Spiritual Growth: Sandalphon is known for assisting individuals in their spiritual growth, helping them to deepen their connection with the divine and understand their true purpose in life.

Communication: Sandalphon is often called upon for assistance in communication, particularly in expressing oneself with clarity and authenticity.

Healing: Sandalphon is believed to have healing powers and can be called upon for physical, emotional, and spiritual healing.

Music: Sandalphon is associated with music and can be called upon for assistance in developing musical abilities and finding inspiration.

Protection: Sandalphon is known for providing protection, particularly for those who are undergoing spiritual and creative processes.

Angelic Connection: Sandalphon is often called upon for assistance in connecting with the angelic realm, helping individuals to receive guidance and support.

Intercession: Sandalphon is believed to intercede on behalf of individuals, helping to bring about positive outcomes and blessings in their lives.

Divine Service: Sandalphon is known for assisting individuals in serving the divine, helping them to find their unique gifts and purpose in life.

Components of a Ritual

The Archangels

The first and main component of your ritual, in our case, will be the selected archangel. We recommend you invoke only one archangel at a time until you are quite familiar with operating rituals. And that, of course, once you have built a relationship with each archangel separately.

While there are so many more than 10 archangels, there are 10 major archangels, as seen before in this book, associated to the 10 planes of consciousness (10 sephiroth of the Tree of Life). While you might have already learned about in the early chapters, let's review them quickly. They each cover specific areas of competence, or influence. Here, we will cover these major archangels.

1- **Metatron**: manifestation, humility, paradoxes.
2- **Ratziel**: esoteric mysteries, gratitude, universal mechanics.
3- **Tzaphkiel**: Divine intelligence, compassion, transformation.
4- **Tzadkiel**: Equity, freedom, forgiveness, justice.
5- **Kamael**: Spiritual influence, moral strength, causality.
6- **Michael**: Personal growth, faith, relationship with God.
7- **Haniel**: Creativity, charity, relationship with nature.
8- **Raphael**: Medicine, prudence, human relationships.
9- **Gabriel**: Revelations, hope, physical energy.
10- **Sandalphon**: Physics and chemistry, simplicity, reality.

Success, health, wealth, protection… many of these topics depend on your personal interpretation and objective. They might involve more than one archangel. We will explain some of these topics and provide examples so you can build your own ritual.

Success is a multifaceted concept that varies greatly from person to person, shaped by individual experiences, values, and aspirations. For some, success may be measured by material wealth and professional achievements, while for others, it could be defined by the ability to maintain fulfilling relationships and personal well-being. Each person's unique perception of success is influenced by cultural, social, and personal factors that mold their priorities and desires. As we navigate through life, it is essential to appreciate and respect the diverse interpretations of success, understanding that what might be a milestone for one person could be insignificant for another.

Since we already covered each archangel in their own chapters. Let us move on to the many other concepts that you might, or might not want to add to your ritual planification. We will cover many components, some of which might surpass your esoteric knowledge. Don't worry about it. We include all of these for the advanced occultist, and the neophyte may very well only consider the concepts and tools easy for them to grasp.

Colors

Colors have a profound effect on the human mind. They can evoke emotions, affect our moods, and even alter our behavior. From the vibrant hues of a sunset to the muted tones of a winter sky, each color holds a unique power over our psyche.

Red, for instance, is a color of passion and energy. It can stimulate the senses and increase heart rate, making it a popular choice for advertising and marketing. It is also associated with danger and warning, which is why it is often used for stop signs and traffic lights.

Orange is often seen as a warm and welcoming color that can promote feelings of happiness, enthusiasm, and optimism. Orange can also stimulate creativity and provide a sense of energy and vitality. In addition, studies have shown that the color orange can increase appetite and boost digestion, which is why it is often used in restaurants and food advertisements. The color is also thought to have a soothing effect on the body and mind, promoting relaxation and reducing stress levels. Overall, the color orange has a bright and uplifting quality that can have a positive impact on one's mood and well-being.

Yellow, on the other hand, is a color of optimism and happiness. It is said to stimulate the intellect and increase mental agility, making it a popular choice for learning environments. It is also associated with caution and warning, which is why it is often used for caution signs and traffic signals.

Green is a color of balance and harmony. It is said to have a calming effect on the mind and body, making it a popular choice for hospitals and healing environments. It is also associated with nature and growth, which is why it is often used for eco-friendly products and sustainable businesses.

Blue (bright or sky blue) is a color of calm and serenity. It can induce feelings of relaxation and tranquility, making it a popular choice for spas and wellness centers. It is also associated with trust and security, which is why it is often used for police uniforms and bank logos.

Indigo (deep dark blue) is a deep and rich color that is often used to represent wisdom, intuition, and perception. Indigo is also considered a calming and soothing color, with the ability to promote relaxation and reduce anxiety. The color has been associated with spirituality and mysticism, and it is often used in meditation and other spiritual practices to help connect individuals with their inner selves. Indigo is also believed to stimulate the imagination and encourage creativity, making it a popular choice for artists and designers. Additionally, the color is associated with honesty and integrity, and it is believed to promote a sense of integrity and responsibility in those who surround themselves with it. Overall, the color indigo has a positive and calming effect on the mind and body, and it is often used to promote emotional balance and well-being.

Purple is considered a symbol of creativity, imagination, and spirituality, and is often associated with luxury, royalty, and elegance. The color is known for its calming effect, and it has been used in meditation and relaxation practices for centuries. It is believed that purple can stimulate the imagination and encourage a sense of creativity, helping people to express themselves more freely. Additionally, purple has been linked to feelings of compassion, empathy, and understanding, making it an ideal color for promoting emotional healing and well-being. Some studies have also suggested that the color purple can help to reduce anxiety and promote a sense of inner peace, which can be beneficial for individuals who are dealing with stress or other mental health issues. Overall, the color purple has a positive and uplifting quality that can have a powerful impact on our emotional and psychological state.

The color **white** is considered a symbol of purity, cleanliness, and innocence. White is known for its calming effect and can create a sense of peace and relaxation. It can also promote feelings of simplicity, clarity, and freshness. In many cultures, white is a color associated with new beginnings and represents a blank slate or a fresh start. White is also believed to have a spiritual quality, representing a connection with a higher power or a divine presence. Additionally, white can promote feelings of openness and purity, helping individuals to let go of negative emotions and thoughts. Overall, the color white has a positive and uplifting quality that can have a powerful impact on our emotional and psychological state, promoting feelings of peace, purity, and renewal.

While it may seem like a negative or dark color, **black** is also considered a symbol of power, sophistication, and elegance. It can create a sense of mystery and intrigue and can be used to create a dramatic and striking visual effect. Black can also represent strength, resilience, and perseverance, as it is a color often associated with survival and overcoming challenges. In many cultures, black is used in clothing and fashion to create a slimming and flattering effect, boosting confidence and self-esteem. Additionally, black can create a sense of calm and stability, providing a sense of grounding and security. Overall, the color black has a complex and multifaceted impact on our emotional and psychological state, promoting feelings of power, sophistication, and strength, as well as providing a sense of calm and stability.

Gray is considered a symbol of balance, neutrality, and calmness. Gray is known for its calming effect and can create a sense of peace and relaxation. It can also promote feelings of stability, reliability, and dependability. In many cultures, gray is a color associated with wisdom and maturity, representing experience and knowledge. Gray is also believed to have a grounding effect, providing a sense of stability and security. Additionally, gray can create a sense of sophistication and elegance, and it is often used in fashion and design to create a timeless and classic look. Overall, the color gray has a positive and calming quality that can have a powerful impact on our emotional and psychological state, promoting feelings of balance, stability, and sophistication.

The colors **olive green** and **brown** are often associated with a grounding psychological effect. Both colors are associated with nature, and they can create a sense of stability, security, and rootedness. Olive green is a color often associated with growth and vitality, representing the natural world and the cycle of life. It can promote feelings of balance and harmony, and it is often used in interior design to create a sense of calm and relaxation. Brown, on the other hand, is a color often associated with earth and soil, representing stability and groundedness. It can create a sense of warmth and comfort, and it is often used in clothing and fashion to create a natural and organic look. Both colors can have a soothing and calming effect on the mind and body, promoting a sense of balance and stability. Overall, the colors olive green and brown have a grounding psychological effect that can promote feelings of connection with the natural world and provide a sense of stability and security.

Each color has its own unique properties and can have a profound impact on our psychological well-being. By understanding the power of color, we can use it to our advantage, whether in our personal lives or in the world of business and marketing. So next time you see a color, take a moment to consider its impact on your mind and how you can use it to achieve your desired outcome.

No need to remember all of these colors and concepts by heart. In the correspondence part of each archangel, we will provide you with the best color to associate with each archangel. Each specific archangel is not necessarily of that color; rather, these are the colors a human ritualist should focus on to better invoke the divine intervention of the desired archangel.

Numerology and gematria

Numerology and Hebrew gematria are both systems that assign numerical values to letters and words in order to gain insight into their meaning and significance. However, there are some key differences between the two systems.

Numerology is a more general term that refers to the study of numbers and their influence on our lives. It is based on the idea that numbers have a vibrational energy that can be used to understand our personality traits, life path, and even predict the future. In numerology, letters are assigned a numerical value based on their position in the alphabet, and these values can be added together to create a single-digit number that represents the essence of a person or thing.

Hebrew gematria, on the other hand, is a specific system of assigning numerical values to Hebrew letters and words. It is based on the idea that each letter has a spiritual significance and that the numerical value of a word can reveal deeper insights into its meaning. In gematria, the numerical value of a word is calculated by adding up the numerical value of each of its letters. This system is commonly used in Jewish mysticism to study the Torah and other religious texts. The names of archangels have been written differently throughout history, even in the same tradition. The spelling and gematria we provide in this book is for reference only. We will use here the ones we use ourselves.

One of the key differences between the two systems is their origin and cultural context. Numerology is a more modern system that has evolved over time and is used in a variety of different spiritual and metaphysical traditions. Hebrew gematria, on the other hand, is rooted in the ancient Jewish mystical tradition and is specifically designed to study Hebrew texts.

Another difference is the way in which the numerical values are assigned. In numerology, letters are usually assigned a value based on their position in the alphabet, whereas in gematria, the values are based on a more complex system of correspondences between letters, numbers, and spiritual concepts.

While both numerology and Hebrew gematria use numerical values to gain insight into the deeper meaning of words and concepts, they differ in their origin, cultural context, and the specific methods they use to assign these values. We won't provide a full course on gematria in this book, but we will provide the gematria value of each archangel, to supplement your knowledge and maybe inspire a few.

Let's review here, what we can say about each decimal number according to modern numerology. We will provide the usual qualities and characteristics, which in a sense, have been extracted from the more esoteric and mystical meaning.

Zero

In numerology, the number 0 is often seen as a symbol of infinity, wholeness, and the potential for new beginnings. It is considered a powerful and mystical number that represents the void or the infinite.

The numerology of 0 is characterized by a strong emphasis on potential and possibility. Individuals who align with this number tend to be open-minded, receptive, and aware of the unlimited potential that exists within themselves and the universe.

The main aspects of the numerology of 0 include:

- Potential: Those with a strong connection to the number 0 tend to believe in the limitless potential of themselves and others. They may be drawn to careers or lifestyles that involve personal growth, self-discovery, or spiritual development.

- Wholeness: The numerology of 0 emphasizes the importance of recognizing and embracing the interconnectedness of all things. Individuals who resonate with this number tend to see the world as a unified whole, with each part being integral to the larger picture.

- Infinity: Those associated with the number 0 often have a sense of awe and wonder about the universe and its infinite possibilities. They may be drawn to exploring the mysteries of the cosmos or delving into the depths of the human psyche.

- New beginnings: The numerology of 0 is often associated with the potential for new beginnings and fresh starts. Individuals who align with this number may be drawn to making significant changes in their lives, whether it be starting a new career, ending a toxic relationship, or embarking on a spiritual journey.

Overall, the numerology of 0 is all about recognizing the unlimited potential that exists within ourselves and the universe. It encourages individuals to embrace change, seek out new beginnings, and recognize the interconnectedness of all things. While it may be a mysterious and elusive number, it offers a sense of possibility and wonder that can be deeply transformative.

This being said, the mystics will see in number 0 the emptiness, the vacuity, the absence of manifestation, from which all potential can rise.

One

Numerologists consider the number 1 to be a powerful and creative force. It is associated with new beginnings, leadership, independence, and self-confidence.

The number 1 is often referred to as the "number of initiation" because it represents the start of a new cycle or venture. It is also seen as a symbol of individuality and originality, as it is associated with being a trailblazer and taking risks.

The main aspects of the numerology of 1 include:

- Leadership: Individuals associated with the number 1 are often natural leaders who are able to inspire and motivate others to follow them. They are confident in their abilities and are not afraid to take charge.
- Independence: Those with a strong connection to the number 1 tend to be independent thinkers who are not easily swayed by the opinions of others. They are self-motivated and prefer to carve their own path in life.
- Creativity: The number 1 is often associated with creativity and innovation. Individuals who resonate with this number may have a strong desire to express themselves through art, music, or other forms of self-expression.
- Courage: The numerology of 1 is also associated with courage and determination. Those who align with this number are often willing to take risks and push themselves outside of their comfort zones in pursuit of their goals. However, we might associate courage also to number 5, depending on the context.

Overall, the numerology of 1 is all about taking charge of your life and blazing your own trail. It is a powerful and dynamic force that encourages you to be bold, creative, and confident in yourself and your abilities.

In mystical kabbalah, the number 1 is also associated to the Creator, the origin of all things pre-manifestation.

Two

In numerology, the number 2 is often associated with balance, harmony, diplomacy, and relationships. It is considered a feminine number, and is associated with the moon and the element of water.

The numerology of 2 is characterized by a strong emphasis on cooperation, teamwork, and partnership. Individuals who align with this number tend to be highly intuitive, empathetic, and sensitive to the needs of others. They value relationships and are skilled at navigating interpersonal dynamics.

The main aspects of the numerology of 2 include:

- Diplomacy: Those with a strong connection to the number 2 are often skilled at resolving conflicts and negotiating solutions that work for everyone involved. They have a natural talent for finding common ground and facilitating compromise.
- Cooperation: The numerology of 2 emphasizes the importance of working together and collaborating with others. Individuals who align with this number tend to be team players who value the input and contributions of others.
- Sensitivity: Those associated with the number 2 are often highly empathetic and intuitive. They have a strong emotional intelligence and are able to pick up on the subtle nuances of interpersonal dynamics.

- Balance: The numerology of 2 emphasizes the importance of finding balance and harmony in all aspects of life. Individuals who align with this number tend to value peace and stability, and may strive to create a sense of calm and order in their environments.

Overall, the numerology of 2 is all about finding balance and harmony in relationships and in life. It encourages cooperation, diplomacy, and empathy, and emphasizes the importance of valuing the contributions of others.

In mystical kabbalah, the number 2 also is associated to duality and paradoxes, to the whole of creation (after 1, the Creator), and all things manifest.

Three

Our numerologist friends will describe the number 3 as often associated with creativity, self-expression, joy, and optimism. It is considered a powerful and positive number that represents growth, expansion, and abundance.

The numerology of 3 is characterized by a strong emphasis on communication, both verbal and non-verbal. Individuals who align with this number tend to be charismatic, expressive, and outgoing, with a natural talent for connecting with others.

The main aspects of the numerology of 3 include:

- Creativity: Those associated with the number 3 often have a strong desire to express themselves creatively, whether through art, music, writing, or other forms of self-expression.

- Communication: The numerology of 3 emphasizes the importance of clear and effective communication. Individuals who align with this number tend to be skilled at expressing themselves and connecting with others.
- Optimism: Those with a strong connection to the number 3 tend to have a positive and optimistic outlook on life. They believe in their own abilities and see the world as full of possibilities.
- Joy: The numerology of 3 is associated with a sense of playfulness and joy. Individuals who resonate with this number often have a good sense of humor and enjoy making others laugh.

Overall, the numerology of 3 is all about creative self-expression, effective communication, and a positive outlook on life. It encourages individuals to tap into their natural talents and abilities, and to share their unique gifts with the world.

In mystical kabbalah, the number 3 is also associate with Divine Intelligence, and the virtue of compassion, which is the highest level of Intelligence, in a spiritual sense.

Four

In numerology, the number 4 is often associated with stability, practicality, hard work, and structure. It is considered a grounded and reliable number that represents the foundation of life.

The numerology of 4 is characterized by a strong emphasis on structure, order, and routine. Individuals who align with this number tend to be practical, dependable, and hard-working, with a strong sense of responsibility.

The main aspects of the numerology of 4 include:

- Stability: Those with a strong connection to the number 4 tend to value stability and security. They are often diligent and disciplined, and may work hard to create a stable and secure life for themselves and their loved ones.
- Practicality: The numerology of 4 emphasizes the importance of practicality and common sense. Individuals who align with this number tend to be grounded and realistic, with a focus on what is feasible and achievable.-
- Hard work: Those associated with the number 4 are often known for their strong work ethic and dedication. They are not afraid of putting in the time and effort necessary to achieve their goals.-
- Structure: The numerology of 4 emphasizes the importance of structure and order in all aspects of life. Individuals who resonate with this number tend to value routine and organization, and may thrive in environments that offer clear guidelines and expectations.

Overall, the numerology of 4 is all about building a strong foundation for success. It encourages individuals to work hard, stay grounded, and create structure and stability in their lives. While it may not be the most exciting number, it is one that provides a solid base for growth and achievement.

In mystical kabbalah, 4 is also associated with manifestation and the desire to make a project more concrete.

Five

In numerology, the number 5 is often associated with change, adaptability, freedom, and adventure. It is considered a dynamic and energetic number that represents movement and evolution.

The numerology of 5 is characterized by a strong emphasis on freedom and flexibility. Individuals who align with this number tend to be adventurous, independent, and open-minded, with a natural curiosity about the world around them.

The main aspects of the numerology of 5 include:

- Change: Those with a strong connection to the number 5 tend to embrace change and see it as an opportunity for growth and evolution. They are not afraid of trying new things and exploring different possibilities.
- Adaptability: The numerology of 5 emphasizes the importance of adaptability and flexibility. Individuals who resonate with this number tend to be able to adjust to changing circumstances and thrive in environments that require them to think on their feet.
- Freedom: Those associated with the number 5 often value freedom and independence. They may be drawn to careers or lifestyles that allow them to be their own boss and live life on their own terms.
- Adventure: The numerology of 5 is associated with a sense of adventure and exploration. Individuals who align with this number tend to be curious and open-minded, with a desire to experience all that life has to offer.

Overall, the numerology of 5 is all about embracing change and living life to the fullest. It encourages individuals to be adaptable, independent, and open-minded, and to approach life with a sense of adventure and curiosity. While it may not always be the most stable or predictable path, it offers a sense of excitement and possibility that is hard to resist.

In mystical kabbalah, 5 is associate also to causality (the non-judgemental idea of karma), moral strength and perseverance.

Six

In numerology, the number 6 is often associated with love, harmony, balance, and service. It is considered a nurturing and caring number that represents the home, family, and community.

The numerology of 6 is characterized by a strong emphasis on relationships and a desire to create harmony and balance in all areas of life. Individuals who align with this number tend to be compassionate, empathetic, and focused on the needs of others.

The main aspects of the numerology of 6 include:

- Love: Those with a strong connection to the number 6 tend to value love and relationships above all else. They may be drawn to careers or lifestyles that involve caring for others, such as nursing, teaching, or social work.
- Harmony: The numerology of 6 emphasizes the importance of creating harmony and balance in all areas of life. Individuals who resonate with this number tend to be skilled at resolving conflicts and creating a sense of peace in their environments.
- Responsibility: Those associated with the number 6 often have a strong sense of responsibility and may take on caregiving roles within their families or

communities. They are reliable and trustworthy, and tend to take their commitments very seriously.

- Service: The numerology of 6 is associated with a desire to serve others and make a positive impact on the world. Individuals who align with this number tend to be altruistic and may be drawn to volunteer work or other forms of community service.

Overall, the numerology of 6 is all about creating loving and harmonious relationships, both within oneself and with others. It encourages individuals to be responsible, caring, and compassionate, and to strive for balance and harmony in all aspects of life.

The mystics will see in the number 6 the concept of wisdom acquired through experience. It is mostly via our relationships that we learn the secrets of love, harmony, responsibility and life in a more philosophical sense.

Seven

In modern numerology, the number 7 is often associated with wisdom, spirituality, intuition, and analysis. It is considered a mystical and mysterious number that represents the search for deeper meaning and understanding.

The numerology of 7 is characterized by a strong emphasis on introspection and contemplation. Individuals who align with this number tend to be analytical, reflective, and introspective, with a natural curiosity about the world around them.

The main aspects of the numerology of 7 include:

- Wisdom: Those with a strong connection to the number 7 tend to value knowledge and wisdom above all else. They may be drawn to careers or lifestyles that involve intellectual pursuits, such as research or academia.

- Spirituality: The numerology of 7 emphasizes the importance of spiritual growth and development. Individuals who resonate with this number tend to be interested in exploring the deeper mysteries of life and may be drawn to meditation, prayer, or other forms of spiritual practice.

- Intuition: Those associated with the number 7 often have a strong intuition and may rely on their inner guidance when making decisions. They are often skilled at reading between the lines and picking up on subtle cues.

- Analysis: The numerology of 7 is associated with a love of analysis and problem-solving. Individuals who align with this number tend to be logical and rational thinkers, with a natural talent for breaking complex problems down into their component parts.

Overall, the numerology of 7 is all about seeking deeper understanding and meaning in life. It encourages individuals to be introspective, analytical, and spiritually aware, and to trust their intuition when making decisions. While it may not always be the most practical or pragmatic approach to life, it offers a sense of depth and richness that is hard to find elsewhere.

Eight

In numerology, the number 8 is often associated with success, power, ambition, and material wealth. It is considered a strong and powerful number that represents abundance and achievement.

The numerology of 8 is characterized by a strong emphasis on material success and achievement. Individuals who align with this number tend to be driven, ambitious, and focused on achieving their goals.

The main aspects of the numerology of 8 include:

- Success: Those with a strong connection to the number 8 tend to be highly motivated and driven to achieve success in their careers and other areas of life. They are often willing to put in the hard work and dedication necessary to achieve their goals.
- Power: The numerology of 8 emphasizes the importance of power and influence. Individuals who resonate with this number tend to be confident and assertive, with a natural talent for leadership.
- Ambition: Those associated with the number 8 often have a strong sense of ambition and may be drawn to high-profile careers or positions of authority. They are not afraid of taking risks or pushing themselves outside of their comfort zones.
- Material wealth: The numerology of 8 is associated with material wealth and financial abundance. Individuals who align with this number tend to be financially savvy and may be drawn to careers in finance, business, or entrepreneurship.

Overall, the numerology of 8 is all about achieving success and abundance in all areas of life. It encourages individuals to be driven, ambitious, and financially savvy, and to use their power and influence for the greater good. While it may be a materialistic and sometimes ruthless approach to life, it offers the potential for great success and achievement.

The mystical adept will understand that the number 8 represents the mind and all its functions. It will thus also cover medicine, the technical and mechanical understanding of all things, and the complex intricacies of "systems", which is required if you wish to achieve success, to manifest your ambitions.

Nine

In numerology, the number 9 is often associated with compassion, philanthropy, humanitarianism, and spiritual awareness. It is considered a selfless and compassionate number that represents the completion of a cycle.

The numerology of 9 is characterized by a strong emphasis on serving others and making a positive impact on the world. Individuals who align with this number tend to be empathetic, compassionate, and focused on the needs of others.

The main aspects of the numerology of 9 include:

- Compassion: Those with a strong connection to the number 9 tend to have a deep sense of compassion for others. They may be drawn to careers or lifestyles that involve helping others, such as social work or nonprofit work.
- Humanitarianism: The numerology of 9 emphasizes the importance of making a positive impact on the world. Individuals who resonate with this number tend to be focused on creating positive change and making the world a better place.
- Spiritual awareness: Those associated with the number 9 often have a strong sense of spiritual awareness and may be drawn to exploring the mysteries of the universe or engaging in spiritual practices.

-   Completion: The numerology of 9 is associated with the completion of a cycle. Individuals who align with this number may be at a point in their lives where they are wrapping up one phase and preparing to begin another.

Overall, the numerology of 9 is all about serving others and making a positive impact on the world. It encourages individuals to be compassionate, empathetic, and spiritually aware, and to use their skills and talents to make a difference in the lives of others. While it may not offer the same material success or power as other numbers, it offers a sense of fulfillment and purpose that is hard to find elsewhere.

We must consider that Compassion will often find a way into many different correspondences, why it is present also in many numbers of numerology. Compassion is an extremely wide field of study and experience. The number 9 will be seen by the mystical kabbalist as the seat of power of the body, the vital plane, and the sexual organs.

This sums up our section on numerology. You won't need to become an expert in numerology to perform your rituals with success. We will provide numerological and gematria numbers for each archangel.

Symbols

Symbols play a significant role in both religious and occult rituals. In many religions, symbols are used to represent concepts, ideas, or entities that are important to the faith. For example, the Christian cross is a symbol of the sacrifice made by Jesus Christ, while the Star of David is a symbol of Judaism.

In occultism, symbols are often used to represent specific intentions, energies, entities, or spiritual forces. Mages and witches are known to use the pentagram as connection to spiritual power. These symbols are believed to have a powerful effect on the practitioner, and they are often used in rituals to invoke or channel these energies. For example, the pentagram is a common symbol in occultism, representing the five elements of earth, air, fire, water, and spirit. Other objects are often arranged in specific patterns or shapes to create a sacred space and enhance the energy of the ritual.

In both religious and occult contexts, symbols can be used to convey complex ideas or spiritual concepts in a simple and accessible way. They can also serve as a focal point for meditation or contemplation, helping practitioners to connect with the divine or spiritual realm. Invoking the help of archangels could be considered both a religious and occult practice. Yet you should not pay attention to these two labels, as what matters is your main intentions, and the actions you will perform to manifest them.

Point

In esoteric or spiritual traditions, a point can represent different concepts depending on the context. One interpretation of the symbol of a point is that it represents the center of consciousness or the source of all creation. This idea is often associated with the concept of the "third eye," which is said to be the seat of spiritual intuition and perception.

Another interpretation is that the point represents the singularity or the moment of creation. In this sense, the point symbolizes the beginning of all things and the potential for infinite expansion. In some traditions, the point is also associated with the element of fire, which represents transformation and purification. The point can be seen as a spark of divine inspiration that ignites the flame of spiritual awakening.

Overall, the symbol of a point can represent many different ideas in esoteric and spiritual traditions, but it often points to the idea of a central, unifying force that underlies all of creation.

Circle

The circle is a powerful and versatile symbol that has been used in esoteric and spiritual traditions throughout history. It represents a wide range of concepts, including wholeness, completion, unity, and the infinite and eternal nature of the universe. The circle can also symbolize the cyclical nature of life and the changing seasons, as well as protection and containment of sacred space. Some traditions associate the circle with the divine or spiritual energy that connects all living beings and the timeless nature of the soul. The circle is a fundamental symbol that points to the interconnectedness of all things and the infinite potential of the universe.

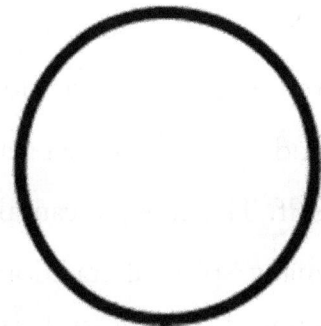

Sphere

The sphere is an esoteric symbol that represents unity, wholeness, and completeness. It is a three-dimensional version of the circle, with no beginning or end, and is often used to represent the infinite and eternal nature of the universe. The sphere can symbolize the interconnectedness of all things, as well as the cyclical nature of life and the changing seasons. In some traditions, the sphere represents the divine or spiritual energy that permeates all of creation, as well as the unifying force that connects all living beings. It can also symbolize the perfection and balance of the universe, as well as the infinite potential of the soul. A crystal ball can represent a sphere.

Triangle

One of its most common interpretations is that it represents the threefold nature of existence - body, mind, and spirit - and the balance between these aspects of the self. The triangle can also represent the divine trinity in many spiritual traditions, such as the Father, Son, and Holy Spirit in Christianity or the Trimurti of Brahma, Vishnu, and Shiva in Hinduism. In some esoteric systems, the triangle is associated with the element of fire, which represents transformation and purification. The upward-pointing triangle is often seen as a symbol of aspiration and spiritual growth, while the downward-pointing triangle can represent the descent into the physical world and the manifestation of spiritual energy in the material realm. The triangle is a versatile and

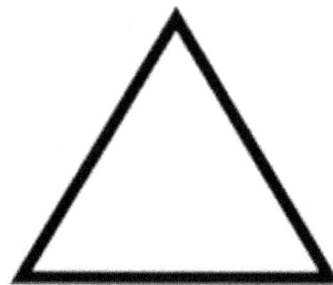

powerful symbol that can be used to represent a wide range of esoteric and spiritual concepts, including balance, transformation, and the divine trinity.

Square

The most grounding symbol, the square is an esoteric symbol that represents stability, order, and balance. Its four sides and corners suggest a sense of symmetry and predictability, making it a symbol of rationality and material existence. In some spiritual traditions, the square is associated with the physical plane and the material world, representing the stability and solidity of the earth element. The square can also represent the four elements of nature - earth, air, fire, and water - and the balance and integration of these forces within the universe. Additionally, the square can symbolize the four cardinal directions - north, south, east, and west - and the idea of completeness or wholeness. In some esoteric systems, the square is seen as a symbol of grounding and protection, as well as a representation of the individual self and the boundaries that define it. The square is a powerful and versatile symbol that can be used to represent a wide range of concepts related to stability, balance, and material existence.

Cross

The cross is an esoteric symbol that has been used in many different cultures and spiritual traditions throughout history. Its most common interpretation is that it represents the intersection of the material and spiritual planes, with the vertical line representing the divine or spiritual energy and the horizontal line representing the physical or material world. The cross is also associated with the concept of sacrifice, as it is said to represent the sacrifice of the ego or the lower self in order to connect with the divine. In Christianity, the cross is a symbol of the crucifixion and resurrection of Jesus Christ, and represents the redemption and salvation of humanity. The four points of the cross can also represent the four elements - earth, air, fire, and water - and the four cardinal directions - north, south, east, and west - as well as the balance and integration of these forces within the universe. Additionally, some esoteric traditions associate the cross with the idea of the eternal or timeless, as it represents the intersection of the past, present, and future.

Pentagram

The upright pentagram is an esoteric symbol that is often associated with magic and the occult. It consists of a five-pointed star with a single point facing upwards, and is said to represent the microcosmic human being standing within the macrocosmic universe. Each of the five points of the pentagram represents an element - earth, air,

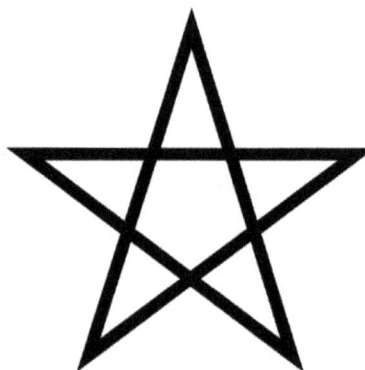

fire, water, and spirit - and their interrelationships within the cosmos. The upward-pointing pentagram is often seen as a symbol of spiritual growth and evolution, with the top point representing the higher self and the four lower points representing the four elements that must be balanced and integrated in order to reach enlightenment. In some esoteric traditions, the pentagram is also associated with the concept of protection and warding off negative energies, as well as the idea of manifesting one's desires through magic. The upright pentagram is sometimes referred to as the "good" or "white" pentagram, in contrast to the inverted pentagram, which is often associated with darker or more negative energies.

Star of David

The Star of David, also known as the hexagram or six-pointed star, is an esoteric symbol that has been used in many different cultures and spiritual traditions throughout history. Its most common interpretation is that it represents the union of opposites, with the upward-pointing triangle representing the divine or spiritual energy and the downward-pointing triangle representing the physical or material world. The six points of the star can also represent the six days of creation in Judaism, as well as the six directions of space - north, south, east, west, up, and down. In some esoteric traditions, the Star of David is also associated with the concept of balance and harmony, as well as the idea of the integration of the masculine and feminine energies within the universe. Additionally, the Star of David is often used as a symbol of Jewish identity and is a prominent feature of the Israeli flag.

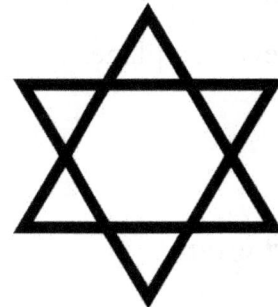

Heptagram

The heptagram, also known as the seven-pointed star, is an esoteric symbol that is often associated with magic and the occult. It consists of a seven-pointed star, with each point representing one of the seven classical planets - the Sun, the Moon, Mercury, Venus, Mars, Jupiter, and Saturn. The heptagram is said to symbolize the harmonious balance and integration of the energies of these planets within the cosmos, as well as the mystical connection between the planets and the human psyche. In some esoteric traditions, the heptagram is also associated with the seven chakras or energy centers of the body, with each point representing one of these centers and their corresponding energies. The heptagram can also be seen as a symbol of protection and warding off negative energies, as well as a tool for invoking or evoking planetary energies in ritual magic.

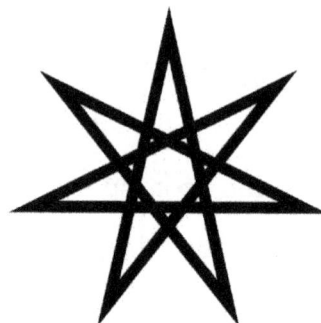

Octagram

The octagram, also known as the eight-pointed star, comes in two variations which hold quite similar meanings. It is an esoteric symbol that is used in many different spiritual and mystical traditions. The first one consists of two overlapping squares, creating an eight-pointed star with each point representing a different concept or element. The second version intertwines its lines in a way to make a

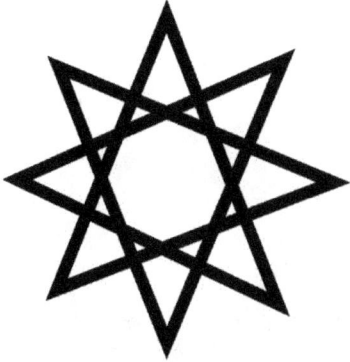

pattern similar to other-grams. It can be used in a more dynamic fashion with its points towards the four directions, or in a symmetric fashion, balancing the forces it represents.

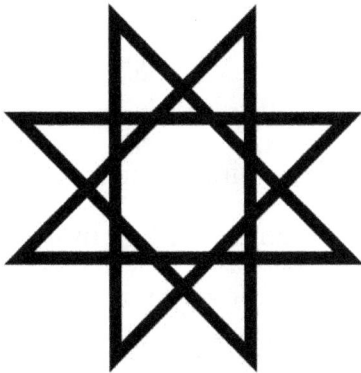

In some esoteric systems, the octagram is associated with the eight directions of the compass - north, south, east, west, northeast, northwest, southeast, and southwest - as well as the balance and integration of these forces within the universe. The octagram can also represent the four classical elements - earth, air, fire, and water - as well as their corresponding qualities of stability, intellect, passion, and emotion. In other traditions, the octagram is associated with the concept of regeneration or rebirth, with each point representing a different phase of the cycle of death and rebirth. The octagram can also be used as a symbol of protection or warding off negative energies, as well as a tool for invoking or evoking elemental energies in ritual magic.

Nonagram

The nonagram, also known as the nine-pointed star, is composed of nine points, arranged in a circular or star-like pattern, and can represent a variety of concepts depending on the context. In some esoteric systems, the nonagram is associated with the nine muses of Greek mythology, representing the arts and inspiration. It can also be seen as a symbol of spiritual enlightenment or attainment, with each point representing a different aspect of the spiritual journey. The nonagram can also be associated with the nine planets of the solar system, as well as the nine-fold nature of the human being - physical, emotional, mental, spiritual, and so on. In other traditions, the nonagram is used as a symbol of protection and defense. It can represent the nine first archangels (excluding Sandalphon) that are said to protect and guide humanity, or the nine spiritual forces that are invoked in ritual magic for protection and purification.

Infinite

The symbol of infinity is an esoteric symbol that represents the limitless, boundless, and eternal nature of the universe. It is often depicted as a horizontal figure eight, with no beginning or end, and is associated with concepts such as eternity, continuity, and unity. The infinity symbol can represent the cyclic nature of life and the interconnectedness of all things, as well as the idea that there is no separation between the material and spiritual planes. In some esoteric traditions, the infinity symbol is associated with the concept of the infinite consciousness, representing the

idea that all beings are interconnected and part of a larger, unified field of consciousness. It can also represent the infinite potential of the human mind and spirit, and the idea that we are capable of achieving spiritual growth and enlightenment beyond our current understanding.

Incense and gems

The previous components of colors, numbers and symbols, where important enough to put directly in the Ritual Component chapter. While it is usual to find incense and semi-precious stones in the arsenal of the ritualist, they are secondary, and we will provide a list in annex, near the end of the book.

Incense sticks vs. censer and coal

Incense sticks and coal censers are both commonly used for burning incense, but they differ in a few key ways. Incense sticks are typically made from a combustible material, such as bamboo, that is coated with fragrant incense. When lit, the incense stick slowly burns down, emitting smoke and fragrance. In contrast, a coal censer uses a small piece of coal or charcoal as the heat source. The coal is lit and placed in the censer, and then the incense is sprinkled on top of the hot coal. As the incense heats up, it releases its fragrance in the form of smoke. One advantage of a coal censer is that it can burn loose incense, while incense sticks are limited to pre-formed shapes. Additionally, a coal censer may provide a stronger scent, as the incense is in direct contact with the hot coal. However, coal censers can be more difficult to use, as they require more attention and care to avoid fire hazards.

Crystals and semi-precious gems

Crystals and semi-precious gems have long been used in various spiritual and metaphysical practices, including occult rituals. These stones are believed to have energetic properties that can be harnessed to enhance the effectiveness of the ritual. Different crystals and gems are believed to have different properties and correspondences with certain intentions or aspects of the self. For example, clear quartz is often associated with clarity, focus, and amplification of energy, while amethyst is associated with spiritual awareness and psychic abilities.

During an occult ritual, crystals and gems may be placed on an altar or worn as jewelry to help align the energy of the practitioner with the intention of the ritual. They may also be used in various ways, such as holding them in the hand, meditating with them, or placing them on different parts of the body.

It's worth noting that the use of crystals and gems in rituals is often based on personal beliefs and practices, and there is no scientific evidence to support their effectiveness. However, many people find them to be a helpful tool in their spiritual practice. We provide, in the annex, a list of common stones.

Symbols and Talismans

In your ritual, you can optionally use symbols to amplify the connection with the archangel, and the type of influence you need. While these are often simply printed on paper, there are many other means to include symbols in your ritual. Objects engraved or that incorporate symbols are called Talismans. These could be engraved in metallic, stone or clay ritual object. They could be carved in a thick leather square, or even on a strap to wear on your body, as a wristband or necklace.

The tools used in a ritual serve as an extension of your intentions and energy. You may choose to craft or purchase these items, but ensure that they resonate with you and align with your spiritual beliefs. Some common tools used in rituals include:

- Phurba (Tibetan vajra knife) or Athame (wicca ritual knife)
- Wand
- Chalice
- Pentacle
- Ritual robes
- Altar cloth
- Sacred jewelry
- Rosary or mala
- Dedicated furniture

Feel free to add tools to this list. When selecting tools, consider their symbolism, energy, and practical use. These could also include personal items that have meaning to you, and in some way correspond to your intention for the ritual.

You may also wish to cleanse and consecrate each item before use to purify and align them with your intentions. You can cleanse your tools with water while reciting mantras or prayers, if said water won't damage the tool itself. You can cleanse your tools by burning incense around it, canting the same mantras or prayers. We recommend you use the same incense you will use for your ritual, unless you are knowledgeable of flavor specific to cleansing ritual tools.

The Art of Rituals

The practice of occult rituals dates back thousands of years, steeped in mystery, symbolism, and arcane knowledge. These rituals have been passed down through generations and continue to evolve, as practitioners adapt to changing times and new understandings. Rather than repeating age-old recipes, we wish to instruction in the art of building your own ritual, as we already started in the early chapters of this book.

In this chapter, we will explore the art of occult rituals, their purposes, common elements, and guidelines for conducting a successful ritual. Occult rituals serve various purposes, including spiritual growth, self-discovery, manifestation of desires, and connection with supernatural entities or energies. They can also be used for healing, protection, or divination. Some common goals of occult rituals include:

- Invoking deities, spirits, or supernatural beings
- Manifesting personal desires, such as wealth, love, or success
- Seeking spiritual growth and enlightenment
- Gaining knowledge and wisdom from higher sources
- Cleansing or purifying one's self or environment
- Developing psychic abilities or honing magical skills

We will first give you guidelines applicable to any kind of occult ritual, and then give precisions on how to apply it to archangels. While the specifics of each type of ritual may differ, most share some common elements:

Education: Study and meditate on every entity, symbol and concept you plan to invoke during your ritual. It doesn't have to be long, but you must have more practice than a 5 minute read.

Planification: With your goal or application in mind, think about all the possible correspondences that you could easily bring together.

Outer Preparation: Cleanse and consecrate your ritual space, gather necessary tools and materials, and prepare yourself mentally, emotionally, and physically.

Inner Preparation: Now that you have gathered your material and tools, it is time to start the ritual, at the appointed time if you had planed this correspondence for your ritual.

Invocation: Calling upon specific deities, spirits, or energies to assist or oversee the ritual. In our case, we invoke the selected archangel, or archangels.

Ritual Performance: Performing symbolic actions and using specific tools to channel energies and manifest the desired outcome.

Offerings: Giving thanks and making offerings to the invoked beings or energies.

Closing: Banishing any unwanted energies, releasing the invoked beings, and closing the ritual space. In our case, we will simply let the archangel go and focus on ourselves.

Guidelines for a Successful Ritual

To increase the effectiveness and potency of your occult rituals, follow these guidelines:

- Establish a clear intention: Know your purpose and desired outcome before starting the ritual, and refine it while planning your ritual.

- Research: Study the deities, spirits, or energies you plan to invoke, as well as the appropriate rituals, tools, and symbols associated with them.

- Personalize your ritual: Adapt and customize the ritual to resonate with your beliefs and personal experiences.

- Respect: Show reverence for the energies or beings you invoke, and handle ritual tools and materials with care and respect.

- Focus and concentration: Engage fully in the ritual, using all your senses and maintaining a focused, meditative state throughout.

- Practice: As with any skill, regular practice will lead to improved results and a deeper understanding of the art of occult rituals.

- Trust your intuition: Listen to your inner voice and follow your instincts, as they may guide you in unexpected ways.

Transmigration mechanics

Whenever you pay attention to something or someone, part of your consciousness, or intentions, goes towards your intended target or interlocutor. This phenomenon is called "Transmigration of Consciousness". The more you focus your mind, heart and will on the process, the more intense will be the transmigration.

When talking to someone, or to some spiritual force, we mostly involve our mind. We usually are less emotionally involved, and there is not much physicality involved. Openly conversing with an archangel will softly send your thoughts its way, and it may come back to you, eventually, with the same softness, mostly affecting your mind.

Praying an archangel will involve your mind, but also your heart, or emotional plane. It is an exclusive period of time, filled with dedication, where your mind is not wandering about. There are more feelings and willpower involved. As you learn to invest yourself fully in a ritual, the results will come to you quicker, and will affect you mentally and emotionally, maybe even physically. During a ritual we perform a lot of physical gestures, and we recite prayers aloud. This helps bring the archangel's influence to the physical plane, and manifest our request.

There are classes of "Transmigration of Consciousness" on my YouTube channel (MahaVajra). These could help you understand the mechanics of the supernatural, spiritual, and ESP.

Education

Early in this book, you've read the chapter on Building a Relationship with the archangels and Empowering Their Names. Invoking archangels is a powerful and transformative spiritual practice that requires adequate knowledge and preparation. Gaining an understanding of each archangel you plan to invoke is essential to maximize the positive effects on both your conscious and subconscious mind. This chapter will discuss the importance of educating yourself about archangels and the impact of reading and meditating on their energies.

Before invoking an archangel, it is crucial to familiarize yourself with their background, attributes, and areas of influence. This knowledge will enable you to establish a strong foundation for your spiritual practice, ensuring that you approach each archangel with respect and reverence. As a result, your connection with the archangel will be deeper and more meaningful, allowing for a greater flow of divine energy and guidance.

Each archangel embodies unique energy patterns and qualities. By studying and understanding these energies, you can align yourself with the archangel's vibration more effectively. This alignment allows you to tap into their divine power and wisdom, leading to profound spiritual growth and personal transformation. Reading about the archangel's qualities and meditating on their energy will enable you to resonate with their frequency and access their guidance more easily.

Educating yourself about archangels helps you develop a clear intention for your invocation. Knowing the specific qualities and attributes of the archangel you wish to invoke allows you to focus your intention and direct your energy towards the desired outcome. A clear intention serves as a powerful compass, guiding you towards a deeper connection with the archangel and enhancing the efficacy of your invocation.

When you read about and meditate on an archangel, your conscious and subconscious mind are both engaged in the learning process. As you absorb the information and internalize the archangel's qualities, your subconscious mind begins to integrate these energies into your being. This integration can lead to profound personal growth, as the archangel's qualities begin to manifest in your thoughts, emotions, and actions.

The practice of educating yourself about archangels and invoking their energies can lead to significant spiritual growth and self-empowerment. By tapping into the divine wisdom and guidance of archangels, you can overcome obstacles, heal emotional wounds, and awaken your innate spiritual gifts. As you continue to learn and grow, your connection with the archangels will deepen, and your spiritual journey will become even more enriching and fulfilling.

Educating yourself about each archangel you plan to invoke is a vital aspect of your spiritual practice. It helps you build a strong foundation, align with the archangel's energy, cultivate intention and focus, and positively impact your conscious and subconscious mind. By dedicating time to reading and meditating on archangels, you will empower yourself to access their divine guidance and wisdom, ultimately leading to profound personal transformation and spiritual growth.

Your ritual education does not only apply to the archangels, but to every mental and spiritual concept you could be using during your ritual. If you aim at becoming a ritualist, we encourage you to study and meditate on every entity, symbol and concept you plan to invoke. This step can take weeks, months, even years, to turn you into an efficient occultist. But you should not wait that long before you do your first practice ritual.

It is totally acceptable to just learn about one archangel, meditate 20 minutes, assemble basic items, and do your first ritual in a jiffy. As you gain experience, you'll want to cultivate a relationship with each major archangel, and do rituals to each of them, keeping a maximum of positive influence in your life.

If you don't intend to become a professional ritualist, it might be too much for you to study and meditate 20 minute per day for years. That is how long it can take to develop all the mental and spiritual tools that you will use in your rituals.

To do a quick empowerment of all these concepts, let's say we meditate one day on each concept. 10 archangels + 10 numbers + 12 symbols + 12 colors and tones = 44 days to get just a basic introduction to each concept. After that, repeat the process with a weeks per concept.

The daily practice consists of reading on the concept, it's meaning and symbolism, followed by a 20 minute meditation.

Amen

You'll be saying "Amen" a lot during your ritual. It is how we finish each invocation, request and gratitude prayer. Amen is an Hebrew word that means "Certainly" or "It is so". Its repeated recitation encourages the manifestation of the spiritual forces you will invoke.

Choosing Your Tools

So many tools are available to furnish your ritual. You don't need all of them. Only one will suffice, but more is better. In addition to at least one tool/object, only the altar is kinda mandatory, unless you are performing outside, making nature your altar.

The altar

Your altar can be as humble as a carboard box covered with an altar cloth, which is also your tablecloth. Or it could be as extravagant as a fully dedicated room with a large table as a permanent central piece.

The altar itself must have a surface of at least a square meter (a square yard), although it need not be square. It actually is more practical if it is rectangular. The example on the right is just an example.

During the ritual your objects, candles and tools will be distributed mostly according to the correspondence of numerology. Some like the elemental standard, which consists of keeping one of each element in the corners. Put earth at the front left, water at the front right, air at the back left, and fire and the back right corner. Even if you have a white candle in the back right corner, you'd still be using a number of colored candles for your ritual, if it's a correspondence you want to add.

Incense, Semi-Precious Stones, and Crystals

Choose incense, stones, and crystals that correspond with the purpose of your ritual. Each element possesses unique properties that can enhance the energy of your ceremony. If you have many crystals, set the smaller ones, or secondary ones, around your altar, while keeping the biggest, or predominant crystal in the main area of the altar. You'll be placing each object either in the 4 corners or the altar, or outside the points of your symbol of choice.

Here are a few examples:

Incense: Sandalwood for purification, lavender for healing, or frankincense for spiritual connection

Semi-precious stones: Rose quartz for love, amethyst for spiritual growth, or black tourmaline for protection

Crystals: Clear quartz for amplifying energy, selenite for cleansing, or citrine for abundance

It's useful to research the properties of each element to determine which best aligns with your ritual's objective. You don't have to become an expert in every esoteric field. You can gather up a ritual in a few minutes with little experience, and it will work. The more study and energy you put in your ritual work, the more powerful then will be.

We provide a short list of incense and crystals with their common use at the end of the book.

Candle Colors and Quantity

Candles are often used to represent specific energies and intentions. Choose colors that correspond with your ritual's purpose. The number of candles may also hold significance, such as using three candles to represent the triple goddess or seven candles for the chakras. In our case, we might want to use a number and color of candles in function of the numerological correspondence of the main angel we are invoking. We understand it might not be comfortable or easy for you to have 10 candles of the rare earthly colors when invoking Sandalphon. Try your best to meet the correspondences you can, and don't worry about those you couldn't.

It is not required to have the number of candles and the color that correspond to your selected archangel. You could chose to have 3 candles for their joyful influence, placed in a triangle as a symbol of the body, mind and spirit. These 3 candles could be blue for freedom, while you are invoking the fifth archangel Kamael, for his determination. This would mix influences from the 3rd, 4th and 5th plane, in addition to all other influences. It might be a bit too many different influences jammed together in a ritual. But if you are out of options, use smaller quantities of objects, and use what you have available at the moment.

While building a relationship with an archangel, and performing a ritual only for the sake of this archangel, we would recommend using all the aspects and correspondences of this archangel. But when you build your ritual, feel free to choose numbers, colors and symbols that fit with your intention, regardless of their apparent differences.

Be careful though, not to combine so many different influences and intentions, that you would end up having what we call a "pizza ritual", composed of so many different influences that each of them is diluted, diminishing the efficiency of your ritual. Try to choose different numbers, colors, symbols, tools, incense, and gems, that each have something to do with your general and most important intention. If you wish for so many different things, we suggest you do multiple rituals at different times, each covering one of your desires.

Various tools

During the ritual performance, you will be using various tools and objects that you brought together, while declaring with clarity your request. You will repeatedly declare your request, prayer or blessing, while handling each tool. Here are examples of what you could do as occult gestures.

4 elements: You might have elected to set up an altar with representations of the elements (such as a candle for fire, a glass of water for water, a feather for air, and a rock for earth), as well as any symbols or objects that relate to the intention of your ritual. During the "invocation" part of the ritual, you could take each elemental symbol in your hand, hold them high in front of you, and recite your invocation. You put it down and take the next elemental object, and do so for each of them.

Incense: You will take your censer or incense stick, and wave it gently around, or even draw a symbol in the air in front of you, all the while reciting your request. Allow the smoke to fill the space, visualizing it carrying your prayers and intentions out into the universe. Note that your censer could also be your air elemental symbol, if you use this system.

Crystals: You might have chosen a crystal that corresponds to the intention of your ritual (such as rose quartz for love, or amethyst for spiritual connection). Take and put the crystal in front of you so you can gaze both at the archangel image and the crystal in the same field of view. You could also put the crystal on a chakra that correspond to your ritual application, and recite your request.

Wand: Use a wand to direct energy during your ritual. Point the wand at different objects on your altar, or use it to draw symbols or sigils in the air to create a magical space.

Chalice: Fill a chalice with water, wine or preferred beverage, and consecrate it as a symbol of the divine feminine. Use the chalice to offer libations to the spirits or deities you are working with, or to bless and consecrate any objects used in your ritual. At the end of your ritual, drink some of the beverage if it is potable.

Tarot Cards: As one of the last steps of your ritual, only if you already are trained with the art of the Tarot, you could draw one or a few cards to gain insight into the situation you are working with. Use the symbolism of the cards to gain clarity and inspiration.

In other words, be creative in the wielding and waving of your ritual tools. You don't need so many tools. Just gather up those you have and go through each of them while reciting your invocation and request prayer.

Planning a Date and Time

The date and time of your ritual can impact the energy and effectiveness of your ceremony. With rituals to archangels, it is recommended to use the times suggested in each correspondence chart. Keep in mind that if you can't fit in the suggested time table, it's only a little influence less to your ritual. It is better to do the ritual at another time, than never do it because of a schedule conflict.

Consider, as an extra minor influence, the following when scheduling:

Moon phases: New Moon for new beginnings, Full Moon for manifestation, and Waning Moon for releasing. Read about the moon phase in detail in the correspondence chart of Gabriel.

Astrological events: Align with the energy of specific planetary alignments, such as Mercury retrograde for communication work. This book not being focused on astrology, we will let you discover this large field of study on your own. We only wanted to add the incentive for those who already have a deep knowledge on astrology. I personally don't have such knowledge.

Creating your Ritual Prayers

Choose prayers, invocations, or chants from your preferred spiritual tradition that resonate with your ritual's objective. These will help you connect with the energies you wish to invoke and enhance the potency of your intentions. We recommend the use of short mantras and prayers that will be easy to repeat multiple times during the ritual.

There are also two short prayers that you will create specifically for your ritual. One is the **invocation prayer**, the other is the **request prayer**. The invocation prayer calls the name of the archangel, and describe his general energy or influence. The request prayer is very specific about your desire or project. Here are some tricks that can help you create your own short prayer:

- Keep it simple: Short prayers can be powerful because they are easy to remember and can be said many times, anytime, anywhere. Keep your language simple and straightforward.

- Focus on a single idea: Rather than trying to cover too many topics in one prayer, focus on a single idea or theme. This could be a request for strength, guidance, or forgiveness, anything that correspond to your ritual intention.

- Use imagery: Adding imagery can help make your prayer more vivid and memorable. For example, you could ask for guidance to be a light in the darkness, or for strength to be a rock in turbulent times. Be poetic yet simple.

- Make it personal: Speak from your heart and use your own words to create a prayer that feels authentic and meaningful to you.

- Be open to inspiration: Inspiration for a prayer can come from anywhere. Keep an open mind and heart, allowing yourself to be moved by the world around you.

Remember, there is no right or wrong way to create a prayer. The most important thing is to speak from your heart and to trust that your words will be heard.

Short mantra

The short mantra is composed of a few words following the name of your selected archangel. It will look like "Mikael the wise" or "Raphael, bestower of health". It is a very short expression that can easily be remembered and will be repeated often in loop during the ritual. When you light the candle and incense, then you position the tools and crystals, whenever you are operating something outside of the invocation and request segment of the ritual, you'll be repeating softly, or even whispering, this short mantra expression.

After selecting your archangel, you'll want to focus on a specific trait of its archetype, or a precise function your will call upon. You can make it as blunt or poetic as you please, as long as it is but a few words.

During charging periods, you'll be taking a minute or more to recite your expression as a way to focus your heart and mind, amplifying the energies invoked during the ritual.

Although I admit, most ritualists practice alone, imagine a few people together whispering slowly, then at increasing speed, "Metatron the Manifestor" asynchronously, filling the space with the mystical presence of Metatron, in a moment of awe for all.

Here is a list of mantra expressions for you to use, if you are not confident in creating your own:

- Metatron, Source of Light
- Ratziel of Revelation
- Tzaphkiel the Compassionate
- Tzadkiel the Just
- Kamael the Strong
- Mikael the Wise
- Haniel the Kind
- Raphael of Medicine
- Gabriel the Messenger
- Sandalphon the Operator

Invocation prayer

The invocation prayer is used as a way to summon the entity you wish to involve in your ritual. It should not contain your direct request, but rather call upon the general blessings this archangel is known to bring. Here are examples of short prayers that can be repeated, as a form of invocation:

"Archangel Michael, please come to me now. Protect me with your sword and shield and surround me with your divine light. Help me to release any fears or doubts and guide me on my path of purpose. Thank you for your love and guidance. Amen."

"Dear guardian angel, thank you for your constant presence in my life. Please guide me with your wisdom and protect me with your love. Help me to trust in the divine plan and to always stay true to my heart's desires. Thank you for your guidance and support. Amen."

"Archangel Raphael, please come to me now. Heal me with your orange light and surround me with your loving energy. Help me to release any physical or emotional pain and guide me towards optimal health and well-being. Thank you for your loving presence. Amen."

The invocation consists in calling the chosen angel to your aid. You will do so by repeating the same, or similar prayer, over a period of 5 minutes. The number of repetitions could coincide with a numerological correspondence, if it is easy to make it so. Otherwise, just repeat it for 5 minutes. Considering you can recite any number of different prayers, you could use your invocation prayer a specific number of times, and fill the remaining period with all the various chants you might have selected. I personally prefer just reciting the invocation prayer, and doing a rosary (or mala) of the archangel name.

Remember, when invoking an angel, that it's important to do so with a humble and sincere heart. Trust that the angelic realm is always available to support you, and allow yourself to receive their guidance and blessings with gratitude.

Create your own prayer, or use one from the tradition of your choice. You will be repeating this request often during the invocation phase. Yet, it is not now that you ask a specific demand. Your invocation should talk of the general benefits you know the angel to bring.

After more or less 5 minutes of invocation, we are now ready to proceed to the ritual, and the main demand, if any.

Request prayer

This request is much more specific than the invocation call. Let's give you one example here, and compare it with the previous invocation prayer:

"Archangel Michael, please help me resolve my conflicts at work. Please bring respect in my workplace. Protect me with your sword and shield, and surround me with your divine light. Help me to release any fears or doubts about my work and colleagues. Please release the negativity from my workplace."

As you can see, part of the request prayer can be quite similar to the invocation prayer, but it now delves much more into the specifics. Let's give another example:

"Dear Tzadkiel, I invoke your power to help manifest my business project of (product or service). Help me plan, and acquire the resources, to make my business real. Help me ground my desire into the world. Amen."

The sacred space

Create a sacred space. Cleanse and consecrate your area using incense smudging, sound, or other preferred methods. You could draw a circle or square to define the boundaries of your ritual space to protect and contain the energies that will be invoked. Not everyone has the luxury of a dedicated ritual space, so you might want to find other means of defining your ritual space in a less permanent way. Some use a large carpet, thin and easy to fold. Others have a thick white linen cord held in place by four dedicated stones, which makes it easy to install and store away.

Some people have a permanent occultum, where they leave most of their ritual material in place. But most of us have our ritual kit in a dedicated and consecrated box. Try to be tidy in the way you store your ritual material.

Material Preparation

Bring together all the items you have prepared in the planification phase.

The place you chose for each item should first answer their functional need, and then answer the symbolic need, when possible. Let's give a few examples: a knife, wand, or masculine symbol should be placed on your right. But if that makes it difficult to use because you are left-handed, put these tools on your left. If, for any reason, your space planning can't accept a censer on your left, put it on your right. As long as every tool is accessible, and when you can, correspond to their symbology, your ritual will go as planned.

If you are not already educated in esoteric symbology, simply follow the instructions given in this book. We don't want to give you specific recipes to follow, but explain to you the concepts required for you to build your own ritual. In this sense, if you feel you are missing information about any aspect of the ritual (where to put a crystal, or with which hand to hold what item), simply follow your intuition. You won't degrade the quality of your ritual but not having absolutely every correspondence that could possibly exist in your ritual. It takes years to cover every single aspect of ritual work. We have provided enough in this book for you to operate successful rituals to the archangels. Trust yourself. Do your best.

Preparing the Ritual

Outer preparation

With your goal or application in mind, think about all the possible correspondences that you could easily bring together. Go through the archangels, or their list of application, and chose wisely which one will help you the most. Pick a symbol, color, number, and if you can, an incense and crystal.

Write down your invocation and request. You should make them simple and precise, unless you are accustomed to poetry, then by all means, indulge in creative expression. The important thing is that the invocation and request are clear.

Make a list of every item you will need to perform the ritual. This will help you gather the items and create the prayers. You don't need all of these, but the more correspondence you join together, the more powerful is your ritual.

- Archangel
- Archangel picture
- Time
- Number
- Symbol
- Color
- Altar cloth
- Candles
- Incense
- Crystal(s)
- Tools

- Offering

- Short mantra

- Invocation

- Request

- …

Proceed to gathering the items. We recommend you put them all in the same place, in a container or already on your altar. The amount of energy invested in the preparation is also going to amplify the effects of your ritual.

How long

The core of the ritual (invocation and request) should last a minimum of 5 minutes, preferably 15 minutes or more. Repeat the steps of your ritual if you feel comfortable doing so. If we consider 5 minutes of meditation, then 5 minutes of initial invocation, add 15 minutes of core ritual looping through your tools, then 5 more minutes for the closing step; it makes for a nice 30-minute ritual. These are only suggestions. You should not calculate the duration of each phase so precisely. The ritual will take the time it needs, as you follow through the steps. If you realize it feels too short for you, repeat the invocation and request phase again.

Offerings

In the realm of occult practices, rituals hold a significant place as they serve as a means to connect with the unseen forces, whether they be spirits, deities, or energies. Although rituals can vary in structure and purpose, one element that is often overlooked but vitally important is the expression of gratitude or thankfulness at the end of a ritual. This chapter aims to delve into the significance of giving thanks and cultivating a sense of gratitude in occult practices.

Expressing gratitude at the end of an occult ritual helps to reinforce and strengthen the connection established between the practitioner and the invoked forces. It demonstrates respect and acknowledgement of the energies, deities, or spirits' presence, solidifying the relationship and fostering trust for future rituals.

In any ritual, the practitioner often asks for assistance, guidance, or manifestation of a specific outcome. By expressing gratitude, one is able to maintain a balance in the exchange of energies, acknowledging that the help received is valued and appreciated. This balance is useful for ensuring continued support and assistance from the forces at play.

An offering could be made to signify this balance, but be warned about the traps of this aspect. What we offer should not uselessly harm a living being. A good example is to throw a pinch of rice and salt in the censor or fire. It is a small quantity that represents sacrifice, but not of any value that could hinder your lifestyle. You could put a fruit on the altar, to then eat it later, or share it with others.

A bad example of sacrifice is to kill a pigeon to the full moon, believing that we are offering life energy. In truth, those who kill animals during a ritual are not offering a life, but are instead taking a life, that they will now owe to the divine forces they were invoking. Blood magic is the best way to become karmically indebted.

However, if an animal would be killed to be eaten anyway, then might as well use that opportunity for making it sacred. This is the premise of the Jewish kosher practice, or the way the Natives who kill their prey by blessing every animal killed for food. Let's say it is not in the reach of most ritualists to kill their food during a ritual. Let us not digress, as I simply felt I had to bring clarity to what we mean by: a small sacrifice.

A grateful mindset can have far-reaching benefits beyond the confines of the ritual space. By regularly practicing gratitude in occult rituals, one can cultivate a broader sense of appreciation for the interconnectedness of all things and the role that unseen forces play in our lives. This shift in perspective can lead to an increased sense of humility, empathy, and openness, improving our overall mental and emotional well-being.

The act of giving thanks can also enhance the efficacy of the ritual itself. Gratitude has the power to raise one's vibrational frequency, which in turn, can attract more positive energies and outcomes. By expressing gratitude, the practitioner may find that their rituals are more potent and successful, as they create a receptive environment for the manifestation of their intentions.

Expressing gratitude at the end of a ritual serves as a respectful way to close the ritual space. It signals to the energies, spirits, or deities that their presence and assistance were appreciated, and that the practitioner is ready to return to their daily life. This respectful closing can help to maintain the sanctity of the ritual space, ensuring that it remains a powerful place for future practices.

Express your gratitude for 3 to 5 minutes. Be calm and relaxed. Recite sporadically thanks to the archangel. Here, you are slowing and calming yourself, slowly crossing into the closing phase of the ritual.

Closing

At the end of the ritual, you will extinguish the candles, close your eyes, and rest for a minute or two. A meditation is indicated, but not necessary. Whatever you do after your ritual, be certain that it won't carry your mind in a negative place. We recommend you don't hop on movie, or tele drama, right after your ritual. Keep your mind clear and peaceful for at least the same duration of your ritual; thus usually another 30 minutes. This calm period allows for the energies called by the ritual, to densify and manifest in the world.

You could decide that a nice walk will help you ground these energies. You could cook your next meal as a symbol of managing resources; maybe even use an ingredient you had on your altar. Putting away the ritual material is a very good way to end a ritual, if you don't intend to use your occultum (ritual space) again soon.

Inner Preparation

Clearing your mind and heart before performing a ritual is essential for several reasons, even if you have the impression you are not successful. First and foremost, it allows you to enter a state of focused awareness and connect more deeply with the energy and intention of the ritual. When you have a cluttered mind or a heavy heart, it can be challenging to fully engage in the ritual's purpose and tap into its transformative potential.

One effective way to clear your mind and heart before a ritual is through a short meditation on the topic of your ritual. This meditation can help you release any distractions or negative emotions that might be holding you back and create a more receptive space for the ritual's energy to flow.

To begin, find a quiet, comfortable space where you won't be interrupted. This should preferably be your ritual space. Sit in a comfortable position, with your back straight yet relaxed. You can use a chair or sit on the floor. Close your eyes and take a few deep breaths, focusing on the sensation of the air moving in and out of your body.

Once you feel grounded, bring to mind the intention of your ritual. Visualize it as vividly as possible, and feel the emotions associated with it. If you're performing a ritual for healing, for example, imagine yourself surrounded by healing light, and feel the warmth and comfort of that light. Don't overexert yourself. We want your mind present, focused and relaxed.

Parasite thoughts will probably show up. Don't worry about it, and keep meditating. As you continue to focus on your intention, notice any thoughts or feelings that arise. If you feel distracted or overwhelmed, simply acknowledge those feelings and let them go. You can imagine them dissolving into the air around you or flowing away like a river. Stay with this meditation for as long as you need, allowing yourself to fully connect with the energy of your intention. When you're ready, take a few more deep breaths and slowly open your eyes.

With your mind and heart clear, you'll be ready to begin your ritual. Whether you're performing a simple meditation or a complex ceremony, approaching it with a focused, open mindset will help you get the most out of the experience.

The Ritual

While this chapter is the one you've been waiting for, it will be the shortest of all chapters, as it simply puts together everything you've learned so far. So let's get right into it.

Cleanse and consecrate your ritual space, gather necessary tools and materials, and prepare yourself mentally, emotionally, and physically.

Place on your altar the tools, candles, crystal, incense, and all the objects you will be using during your ritual. Try to follow the patterns of correspondence, placing objects at different points of your symbol. It is not dramatic if you don't have as many tools as you have numbers. For some, it is either not practical or just not possible to have 9 different tools just because you use a nonagon to call upon Gabriel.

It is time. We finally reached the point where we will perform the ritual. It is good to read and understand every step of the ritual. Read and re-read it if you need. During the ritual itself, you won't have time, or mind, to read again this chapter. We recommend you only use the recapitulation chart provided at the end of this book.

However, it is not dramatic if you miss a step, or don't do everything exactly as it should. It won't have a negative effect in your life. As long as you practice, and do your best, the results will be fine. What could bring negativity in your life is your daily actions. Missing a step in a ritual will simply bring a bit less positivity.

Here are the steps explained, which will be recapitulated later.

Ritual steps

Physical activation: Start the ritual at the time you chose. Start reciting your short mantra, over and over as you light the candles, then the incense.

Meditation: Meditate a few minutes on the topic of your ritual, while reciting your short mantra. Do your best to be non-dramatic about it. While you slowly recite or whisper the short mantra, try to dwell on the general concept of your invocation and request. Focus less on the problem itself, although it should also be present in your mind.

For many, a ritual is mostly to express our tanks, and build a stronger relationship with spiritual forces. But sometimes, it is to ask for help, or for something to happen. You should invest your energy in the result you wish for, and not the pain that currently afflicts you.

Invocation: This step is not meditative. It is time to activate yourself by praying aloud, with your eyes open. Gaze at the picture of the archangel if you have it or read the invocation if you have not memorized it. I never memorize long ritual texts. I simply review them quickly before each step. And it's fine if you hole your text in one hand, and use the other to operate the ritual gestures.

Take each tool you have selected (cup, dagger, censer, main crystal…) and one by one, hover them in front of your altar, drawing your symbol of choice (square, circle, pentagram…). When done with the first tool, put it in its place, bow in gratitude, and take the next one… and so on for all your tools, or for as many repetition that fits in your numerological correspondence.

Request: Recite your request a number of time corresponding to your choice of number (1 to 9) for this ritual. Same as with the invocation, you should use your tools one after the other, while reciting your request. The request part of the ritual is the one you loop over until you have reached enough time.

You can add an extra step, if you have time, once you've gone through all your tools. Slowly touch each of your tools, reciting once your short mantra. Then bring both hands up and chant your short mantra to your archangel a number of time that corresponds to your ritual concept.

Repeat the request cycle as long many times as you see fit.

Offerings: Nearing the end of the ritual, it is time for giving thanks and making offerings to the invoked beings or energies. If you have prepared a small object for the offering, you can throw it in the fire, or spread it on your altar. It should be a small quantity, as it is only a symbol. If you intend to eat the offering, keep it in a bowl or napkin for easy recuperation, simply placing it on your altar.

Recite an improvised thank-you to your archangel. Say "thank you" to your short mantra name, for intervening in your like. Something like "Thank you Michael the wise, for the inspiring wisdom you bring, for your blessings and guidance. Amen."

Closing: Let the archangel go and focus on yourself. Meditate another few minutes, silently or whispering your short mantra.

Ritual Recap

Physical activation: short mantra, light candles and incense

Meditation: short mantra, a few minutes

Invocation: recite invocation while wielding each tool

Request: recite request while wielding each tool, short mantra calling

Offerings: give thanks, place your offering.

Closing: extinguish the candles, relax with positive thinking.

Example rituals

Let's provide you with a few example rituals, from simple to complex. We will start with the quickest and most practical daily ritual, and then offer a much more elaborate ritual example.

Daily Grind Ritual

You can make a ritual to an archangel on a daily basis, just looping through the 10, one each day, and start over again. These rituals could be short and simple to setup, counting on a minimal correspondence, like the number of candles of a certain color.

Recipes

Writing this book, we hoped to avoid writing a recipe book for all to follow blindly, focusing more on training you into the art of rituals, and showing you how to build a relationship with each archangel. However, now that the book is almost done writing, I figure there is a lot to learn before one could create their rituals efficiently. We will hence provide a series of simple recipes that you can follow until you become more competent with each aspect of the ritual art.

In these quick recipes, we won't dive into the tools, crystals and incenses. We'll provide the simplest rituals for you to follow. You'll add to it as you learn, until you can compose your own rituals. We recommend you use a basic incense that you like.

Considering that we don't know exactly what you want to do with these pre-made rituals, the request prayer we provide cannot be precise. We invite you to modify them to fit your needs, or simply use them as a second invocation, which will provide you the general benefits of each archangel.

Metatron מַטַטְרוֹן

Material:

One big white candle

Picture of Metatron

Physical activation: short mantra, light candle and incense

Short mantra: Metatron manifest

Meditation: short mantra, a few minutes

Invocation: repeated recitation a few minutes, hands in prayer or relaxed.

Invocation: "Metatron, herald of creation, I call you, come forth in this place, and make it holy. Master of manifestation, I summon your aid in creating everything spiritual and physical, that I might need along my journey."

Request: recitation a few times, hands and arms open, looking at picture or upwards, then a few confident short mantra calling

Request: "Metatron please bless me with creativity to find solutions to any situation that needs resolving, and with the skills and resources to apply them."

Offerings: give thanks, place your offering.

Closing: extinguish the candles, relax with positive thinking.

Ratziel רְזִיאֵל

Material:

One white and one black candle, or two grey candles.

Picture of Ratziel

Physical activation: short mantra, light candle and incense

Short mantra: Ratziel reveal

Meditation: short mantra, a few minutes

Invocation: repeated recitation a few minutes, hands in prayer or relaxed.

Invocation: "Ratziel, lord of mysteries, I call you, come forth in this place, and make it holy. Master of revelations, I summon your aid in awakening me to wisdom and concepts that I might need along my journey"

Request: recitation a few times, hands and arms open, looking at picture or upwards, then a few confident short mantra calling

Request: "Ratziel, please bless me with deep revelations that would bring peace and joy to my journey."

Offerings: give thanks, place your offering.

Closing: extinguish the candles, relax with positive thinking.

Tzaphkiel צָפְקִיאֵל

Material:

Three purple candles

Picture of Tzaphkiel

Physical activation: short mantra, light candle and incense

Short mantra: Tzaphkiel the compassionate

Meditation: short mantra, a few minutes

Invocation: repeated recitation a few minutes, hands in prayer or relaxed.

Invocation: "Tzaphkiel, lord of compassion, I call you, come forth in this place, and make it holy. Master of the highest virtue, I summon your aid in both receiving and providing compassion, that any might need along their journey"

Request: recitation a few times, hands and arms open, looking at picture or upwards, then a few confident short mantra calling

Request: "Tzaphkiel, please bless me with the humility and confidence to remain in compassion in any situation."

Offerings: give thanks, place your offering.

Closing: extinguish the candles, relax with positive thinking.

Tzadkiel צַדְקִיאֵל

Material:

Four blue candles

Picture of Tzadkiel

Physical activation: short mantra, light candle and incense

Short mantra: Tzadkiel the just

Meditation: short mantra, a few minutes

Invocation: repeated recitation a few minutes, hands in prayer or relaxed.

Invocation: "Tzadkiel, lord of equity, I call you, come forth in this place, and make it holy. Master of the highest justice, I summon your aid in both being treated and treating others with justice along our journey."

Request: recitation a few times, hands and arms open, looking at picture or upwards, then a few confident short mantra calling

Request: "Tzadkiel, please bless me with the humility and integrity to remain in just in any situation."

Offerings: give thanks, place your offering.

Closing: extinguish the candles, relax with positive thinking.

Kamael כַּמָאֵל

Material:

Five red candles

Picture of Kamael

Physical activation: short mantra, light candle and incense

Short mantra: Kamael the strong

Meditation: short mantra, a few minutes

Invocation: repeated recitation a few minutes, hands in prayer or relaxed.

Invocation: "Kamael, lord of strength, I call you, come forth in this place, and make it holy. Master of the highest power, I summon your aid so I might have all the strength needed on my journey."

Request: recitation a few times, hands and arms open, looking at picture or upwards, then a few confident short mantra calling

Request: "Kamael, please bless me with humility and strength so I may be able to face any situation."

Offerings: give thanks, place your offering.

Closing: extinguish the candles, relax with positive thinking.

Mikael מיכאל

Material:

3 or 6 candles, all gold, orange or yellow, or a mix.

Picture of Mikael

Physical activation: short mantra, light candle and incense

Short mantra: Mikael the wise

Meditation: short mantra, a few minutes

Invocation: repeated recitation a few minutes, hands in prayer or relaxed.

Invocation: "Mikael, lord of wisdom, I call you, come forth in this place, and make it holy. Master of the highest intelligence, I summon your aid so I might have all the wisdom needed on my journey."

Request: recitation a few times, hands and arms open, looking at picture or upwards, then a few confident short mantra calling

Request: "Mikael, please bless me with spiritual experiences and growth, so I may be able to understand any situation."

Offerings: give thanks, place your offering.

Closing: extinguish the candles, relax with positive thinking.

Haniel חַנִּיאֵל

Material:

7 green candles. 3 if 7 is too many.

Picture of Haniel

Physical activation: short mantra, light candle and incense

Short mantra: Haniel of Nature

Meditation: short mantra, a few minutes

Invocation: repeated recitation a few minutes, hands in prayer or relaxed.

Invocation: "Haniel, lord of nature, I call you, come forth in this place, and make it holy. Master of the highest charity, I summon your aid so I might have kindness facing any situation."

Request: recitation a few times, hands and arms open, looking at picture or upwards, then a few confident short mantra calling

Request: "Haniel, please bless me so I may treat others, and be treated with kindness, in any situation."

Offerings: give thanks, place your offering.

Closing: extinguish the candles, relax with positive thinking.

Raphael רְפָאל

Material:

8 orange candles. 3 if 8 is too many.

Picture of Raphael

Physical activation: short mantra, light candle and incense

Short mantra: Raphael the erudite

Meditation: short mantra, a few minutes

Invocation: repeated recitation a few minutes, hands in prayer or relaxed.

Invocation: "Raphael, lord of knowledge, I call you, come forth in this place, and make it holy. Master of the highest understanding, I summon your aid so I might have the skills to face any situation."

Request: recitation a few times, hands and arms open, looking at picture or upwards, then a few confident short mantra calling

Request: "Raphael, please bless me with an educative life, with wonderful relationships and activities."

Offerings: give thanks, place your offering.

Closing: extinguish the candles, relax with positive thinking.

Gabriel גַבְרִיאֵל

Material:

9 purple candles. 3 if 9 is too many.

Picture of Gabriel

Physical activation: short mantra, light candle and incense

Short mantra: Gabriel the messenger

Meditation: short mantra, a few minutes

Invocation: repeated recitation a few minutes, hands in prayer or relaxed.

Invocation: "Gabriel, lord of power, I call you, come forth in this place, and make it holy. Master of life, I summon your aid so I might have energy and health along my journey."

Request: recitation a few times, hands and arms open, looking at picture or upwards, then a few confident short mantra calling

Request: "Gabriel, please bless me with spiritual experiences, and the senses to perceive them."

Offerings: give thanks, place your offering.

Closing: extinguish the candles, relax with positive thinking.

Sandalphon סַנְדַּלְפוֹן

Material:

Four candles: green, yellow, blue, brown/black.

Picture of Sandalphon

Physical activation: short mantra, light candle and incense

Short mantra: Sandalphon pervade

Meditation: short mantra, a few minutes

Invocation: repeated recitation a few minutes, hands in prayer or relaxed.

Invocation: "Sandalphon, lord of the world, I call you, come forth in this place, and make it holy. Master of reality, I summon your aid so I might have energy and resources along my journey."

Request: recitation a few times, hands and arms open, looking at picture or upwards, then a few confident short mantra calling

Request: "Sandalphon, please bless me with patience and objectivity in any situation."

Offerings: give thanks, place your offering.

Closing: extinguish the candles, relax with positive thinking.

Annexe

Incense properties

There are numerous varieties and blends of incense, with varying properties. We provide you with an short list of some popular incense types and their associated holistic properties:

Amber incense is known for its calming and balancing effects. It promotes feelings of harmony and peace and enhances love and sensuality.

Benzoin incense helps in uplifting mood, relieving stress, and purifying the surrounding atmosphere.

Cedarwood incense helps with grounding and centering, promoting focus and clarity, and clearing negative energy.

Cinnamon incense is believed to attract prosperity and abundance, boost energy and motivation, and enhance spiritual growth.

Copal incense is used for purifying and cleansing energy, promoting spiritual healing and protection, and strengthening the connection to the divine.

Eucalyptus incense supports respiratory health, clears negative energy and mental fog, and promotes healing and balance.

Frankincense incense deepens meditation and spiritual connection, relieves stress and anxiety, and enhances mental clarity and focus.

Gardenia incense promotes peace, love, and harmony, and can help enhance emotional well-being.

Honeysuckle incense attracts happiness and prosperity, boosts intuition, and encourages spiritual growth.

Jasmine incense encourages love and sensuality, boosts self-confidence, and fosters creativity.

Lavender incense helps to calm and relax the mind, relieve stress and anxiety, and promote restful sleep.

Myrrh incense is used for purification, protection, and enhancing spirituality, and it can also help balance emotions.

Patchouli incense is often used for grounding, attracting love and abundance, and fostering emotional balance.

Rose incense is associated with love, emotional healing, and enhancing creativity and intuition.

Sandalwood incense aids in meditation, relaxation, and spiritual growth, and it can also help to clear negative energy.

Vanilla incense has a calming and soothing effect, encourages self-love and confidence, and fosters mental clarity.

Vetiver incense is grounding and stabilizing, helps with emotional balance, and promotes restful sleep.

Ylang-Ylang incense is known for its sensual and uplifting properties, helping to reduce stress and anxiety and promoting emotional balance.

Gems and crystal properties

Providing an exhaustive list of all crystals and semi-precious gems with their holistic properties is a challenging task, as there are countless varieties, and new ones are continually being discovered. Additionally, holistic properties can vary depending on individual beliefs and cultural backgrounds. However, we wish to provide you with an alphabetical list of some popular crystals and their commonly associated holistic properties. Keep in mind that individual experiences may vary. Some of these stones can become quite expensive, while the same properties might be provided by more accessible alternatives. You should search online for the stones that fit your needs and budget.

Agate: Balance, stability, grounding, and emotional healing

Amazonite: Courage, communication, and harmony

Amethyst: Spiritual growth, intuition, and emotional balance

Apatite: Inspiration, motivation, and communication

Aquamarine: Calming, stress relief, and mental clarity

Aventurine: Luck, abundance, and emotional healing

Azurite: Intuition, insight, and spiritual growth

Bloodstone: Strength, courage, and purification

Calcite: Cleansing, energy amplification, and mental clarity

Carnelian: Creativity, courage, and motivation

Celestite: Spiritual growth, intuition, and angelic connection

Chalcedony: Emotional balance, communication, and harmony

Chrysocolla: Communication, expression, and emotional healing

Chrysoprase: Love, abundance, and emotional healing

Citrine: Abundance, prosperity, and self-confidence

Clear Quartz: Energy amplification, clarity, and healing

Emerald: Love, abundance, and emotional healing

Fluorite: Mental clarity, focus, and spiritual growth

Garnet: Passion, motivation, and grounding

Hematite: Grounding, protection, and mental clarity

Howlite: Calming, stress relief, and spiritual connection

Jade: Prosperity, good fortune, and emotional healing

Jasper: Grounding, stability, and protection

Kyanite: Communication, intuition, and spiritual growth

Labradorite: Intuition, transformation, and spiritual growth

Lapis Lazuli: Intuition, wisdom, and spiritual growth

Larimar: Emotional healing, communication, and stress relief

Lepidolite: Calming, stress relief, and emotional healing

Malachite: Transformation, protection, and emotional healing

Moldavite: Spiritual growth, transformation, and cosmic connection

Moonstone: Intuition, emotional healing, and feminine energy

Obsidian: Protection, grounding, and emotional healing

Onyx: Protection, grounding, and self-confidence

Opal: Creativity, inspiration, and emotional healing

Peridot: Abundance, prosperity, and emotional healing

Prehnite: Spiritual growth, intuition, and emotional healing

Pyrite: Abundance, protection, and self-confidence

Rhodonite: Emotional healing, self-love, and forgiveness

Rose Quartz: Love, emotional healing, and self-love

Ruby: Passion, motivation, and emotional healing

Rutilated Quartz: Energy amplification, spiritual growth, and healing

Sapphire: Wisdom, intuition, and spiritual growth

Serpentine: Spiritual growth, kundalini energy, and emotional healing

Sodalite: Intuition, communication, and emotional balance

Sunstone: Empowerment, self-confidence, and abundance

Tanzanite: Spiritual growth, intuition, and emotional healing

Tiger's Eye: Grounding, protection, and self-confidence

Topaz: Abundance, manifestation, and emotional healing

Tourmaline: Protection, grounding, and emotional healing

Turquoise: Communication, protection, and emotional healing

Unakite: Emotional healing, balance, and spiritual growth

Variscite: Emotional healing, self-confidence, and inner peace

Vesuvianite: Spiritual growth, intuition, and emotional healing

Zircon: Protection, grounding, and emotional healing

Metatron מֶטַטְרוֹן

Ratziel רָזִיאֵל

Tzaphkiel צַפְקִיאֵל

Tzadkiel צַדְקִיאֵל

Kamael כמאֵל

Mikael מיכאל

Haniel חַנִיאֵל

Raphael רָפָאל

Gabriel גַּבְרִיאֵל

Sandalphon סַנְדַלְפוֹן

www.ingramcontent.com/pod-product-compliance
Lightning Source LLC
Chambersburg PA
CBHW050500110426
42742CB00018B/3317